BRAKENSTROOM

BRAKENSTROOM

Stories from South Africa

JACOB SINGER

REGNIS PUBLISHING
2000

Regnis Publishing
2130 Nanton Avenue
Vancouver, B.C. Canada
V6L 3C7
phone 604.263.4427
fax 604.263.4214
email jasin@home.com

Layout and design by the Vancouver Desktop Publishing Centre
Printed in Canada by

CANADIAN CATALOGUING IN PUBLICATION DATA
Singer, Jacob A., 1935-
Short stories from Brakenstroom, South Africa

ISBN 0-9687224-0-7

1. South Africa—History—Fiction. i. Title.
PS 8587.I5529S54 2000 C813'.6 C00-910537-9
PR9199.3S5345S56 2000

Contents

The stories in this book are based on fact, but the characters are fictional.

Introduction

SOUTH AFRICA IS A LAND of immigrants. During the first quarter of the nineteenth century, black tribes were moving from Central Africa southwards down the East Coast while white Dutch settlers from the Cape of Good Hope were moving northwards to escape British rule. The Hottentots and particularly, the Bushmen, the original natives of the country, streamed into the arid areas of the Kalahari to escape genocide.

Many battles were fought between the black tribes and the white migrants as they met head on in their migration. The Voortrekkers, as the Dutch migrants were now called, had many of their pioneers killed as they confronted Dingaan's Zulu empire, but their superior weapons eventually allowed them to overcome the native tribes. They settled in the broad and empty veldt of the Transvaal and Free State. The land was uninhabited, and they laid their claim as they staked their farms. It was during one of these treks that Brakenstroom was founded on the banks of the willowed Brak River; a river which lazily meandered through the red fertile soil offering the farmers plenty of water. They divided the rich veldt amongst themselves (one day's horse ride defining the boundaries of each farm) and began to extensively farm the veldt between the koppies (small hills) that formed the rich fertile valley that became Brakenstroom.

As the infrastructure of the Boer Republik developed, Brakenstroom became a base for exploration into the interior with hundreds of adventurers and prospectors streaming through the town as they explored the surrounding countryside. Diamonds had been found at Kimberley and there was always the possibility of another great diamond find. When gold was discovered on the Witwatersrand ninety-two miles away, and the golden city of Johannesburg was still a congregation of prospector tents, Brakenstroom boomed.

Most of the Jewish emigrants from Europe travelled to America, but the few that came to South Africa were more adventurous, lured by the stories of enormous wealth. Very few made their fortunes on the gold and diamond fields. Most prospered in businesses to service the prospectors and the families that followed them.

This book is a collection of short stories about Brakenstroom and a few of its inhabitants. These are stories that the author heard from his parents and their friends. All are based on truth, but in most instances, a number of personalities have been merged to create a single character; for example, the story about Meish is actually the story of three different men. Life in Koster and the events leading to Koster were the experience of one friend, who relived them while walking on Muisenberg Beach. The story about Emmie, the mayor's wife, and the story of the hearing aid belong to another eccentric of the town, who has even more remarkable stories to his name, while the kidnapping with its earlier events in the Shtetl belong to yet a third unforgettable character.

Notably absent in this book are stories about the black Africans of South Africa. There are plenty of stories that can be told, but I can only touch on the pathos and drama that every black person felt by living in South Africa. To the white South Africans, they were the shadows that kept the house clean, cared for the children, and worked in the fields and gardens. Under white supervision and with white engineers, the black Africans built the cities and towns and worked the mines that brought the country tremendous wealth. Without white technology the black tribes may have remained a tribal empire, warring among each other. With white technology and the oppressive master slave ideology that came with the whites, black Africans became users, rarely innovators. Although they were granted a limited education, they were never given true opportunity, the cornerstone of a viable democracy. It has been said that the greatest tragedy of Africa was colonialism, and the second greatest tragedy was when the colonists left. One has only to look at Africa today to see that with Independence came poverty, hardship, starvation, and in many cases civil war, with the slaughter of millions of innocents. South Africa has yet to prove otherwise, but it's large white population, many fourth, even fifth generation South Africans, may be pivotal in preventing the gradual degradation found in the rest of black Africa.

The reader should remember that at the time these stories took place, Hendrik Verwoerd had not yet become Prime Minister, and the hated apartheid laws that he implemented were not an official part of South African legislation, although racial discrimination was rife and legislation of a discriminatory kind did exist. The black man and the brown man that lived in this pluralistic society were regarded as inferior to the white Baas. Mahatma Gandhi, in the period he lived in South Africa, sharpened the passive resistance knife that he used so effectively in India, on a South African whetstone.

The Boers never colonised South Africa. They simply took it because it was empty and "up for grabs." It was Britain's Cecil John Rhodes who, in establishing a financial empire in Southern Africa, forced Britain to protect his assets and conquer the Boers in the Anglo-Boer war. The war changed many traditions in the British army. Red coats were exchanged for khaki uniforms as their soldiers were easy targets for Boer sharp shooters. Concentration camps that imprisoned women and children of the Boer Commando under ghastly conditions were created because they cared for and fed their husbands and sons while in the field. For the first time in the history of warfare, innocents were confined behind barbed wire and the poor conditions and a shortage of food in the camps led to the deaths of thousands of Boer women and children. The hate that was nourished against England and everything that was English in these camps was the reason why South Africa very nearly entered the Second World War on the side of the Germans. During the Boer War, the Zulus, Xosas, Tswanas, Soesoetoes, Matabeles and other smaller tribes were the spectators.

In the story "Hettie," blacks are mentioned for the first time, and then as heroes and heroines. They saved a young white girl's life. This is the role black women played in white society—they were the comforters, the alternate mothers, and the wetnurses. They were loved, hated, abused and discarded, but they were never feared. Fear only came after their liberation and yet in all the years of terrorist warfare, when they fought for their independence, they never ever attacked or hurt one white child even though they had plenty of opportunity.

Today, they abhor being patronised, yet many of the older blacks still rely on the pensions paid to them monthly by their white employers, and they and their families expect and believe they deserve it as due payment for a lifetime of loyalty.

Are there more stories to be told? Yes, there are plenty more, as there are in any small town in South Africa. There are still the stories of Wendy and John, of Helen and Christopher, and of Mary. There is also the story of Chris and Selma, telling how Chris returned as a ghost with a message to Selma after he had died, and there is the tragic story of Harry, the man who never went outside. These are, however, stories for another book.

Jacob Singer
August 6, 1997

Leonard

LEONARD WAS BORN Leonard Francis Sandler, in the same nursing home at the top of Berg Street that David had been born in and which, at that time, was the only respectable nursing home Brakenstroom had. His parents were originally from Russia, lured to the gold fields of Johannesburg as stories of Africa's riches filtered through the ghettos of Europe.

Leonard's father, Solomon, after eventually arriving in Johannesburg, soon realised that a growing city needed bookkeepers, and so applied his knowledge to auditing other people's businesses. He worked hard, the hours spent pouring over accounting books giving him the stooped scolitic back and chronic myopia that on his tall thin frame, offered a portrait of the Scrooge circumstances had made him. His miserliness lasted until he had saved enough money to buy a small farm in the Brakenstroom district where he began speculating in cattle. With his shrewd business sense, something Leonard never inherited, he became very successful and very wealthy.

Rachel, Solomon's wife, was a simple woman. All who knew her remembered her as the finest baker in town. Her chocolate cake was the best, and her cheesecake—well, David's mouth would water whenever he thought of her golden-topped cakes, even to this day. He could remember the rich cheesy smell that pervaded the house as she took the cakes from the oven. Because of his Mother's baking, Leonard was probably the most popular boy in town, although, to be quite honest, as Mrs. Brick's daughters matured, and boys learned more about girls, Mrs Brick's bagels were sometimes better than the chocolate cake. This more so when they were served with the beautiful smile and fair hand of either daughter holding a plate of hot bagels fresh from the oven, dripping farm butter into mugs of sweet tea as the boys crowded around the kitchen table.

Leonard had inherited his father's looks and his mother's brain. Not that he was simple—far from it. He was always in the top ten at school, but he was simply not the leader he would so dearly have liked to have been. He was always a follower, basking in everyone else's limelight, and whatever his achievements were, came through hard work and dedication. As a boy he was always a head and shoulders taller than others his own age, as thin as a stick, with two large ears on either side of a very Jewish nose. His ears were so big that they earned him the nickname of 'Dumbo' when that famous Disney movie first hit the circuit. Then, as if to make sure he kept his balance and his feet on the ground, nature gave him a size ten foot while he was still in primary school. He was one of those unfortunates who had two left feet and couldn't throw a cricket ball straight no matter how hard he tried. He was simply enormously gawky, but his feet stopped growing and by the time he was seventeen, he still wore a size ten shoe.

David had known him simply forever, or it seemed like forever. He believed that his mother must have invited Leonard to his first birthday party, although he did not know for certain, as he could not remember that far back. He always believed that it must have been so, and Leonard had fostered that belief. Leonard was a year and one month older than David, and was tall, almost a head and shoulders taller than all the other boys of his age. As they grew older, Leonard seemed to shrink, probably as a result of being round-shouldered and the habit he had developed of stooping to be less conspicuous.

David felt that he owed Leonard his life. Brakenstroom had a municipal swimming pool, a short walk from where they both lived. It was an Olympic-sized pool, with wide graceful lawns on either side, set in a park with gardens of red cannas contrasting with the pink or white Pride of India trees in the centre of each flower bed. The gardens were the pride of the town and were a background to the numerous wedding pictures that were photographed on almost every weekend. On the western boundary of the gardens, a small river flowed gracefully between the willow trees that lined its banks, the smooth dark water disturbed into

V-shaped ripples by the long willow branches whose tips trailed in their reflections. What more could any young boy ask for? As children they spent their summer holidays lazing at the pool, making their way from their houses barefoot across the hot tar of the macadam road. The soles of their feet would blister, and in almost unbearable agony and screaming with pain they would jump onto the sun-scorched grass on the pavement*, only to find it interspersed with thorns that mingled with the pain from the hot tar. Then with a sigh of relief, they would dash for the furrow that flowed with cool water down the side of the pavement, often slipping in the algae, and with shrieks of laughter they would lie soaking wet, pulling the thorns from each others' feet.

As teenagers, they later found the willows and the river to be the perfect setting for exploring the opposite sex, with many a girl coming close to losing her virginity in the cool shade, probably seduced more by the gardens than by the fumbling boy next to her.

When David was about six and in Grade One at Bracken Primary School, they were taken as a class to the pool to learn how to swim. David had soon become bored with the lesson. Seeing Leonard at the deep end, he had gradually worked his way around the side of the pool to where Leonard played. Unfortunately for him, a steel ladder was attached to the side of the pool wall, and in working his way around it, he had lost his grip. He remembered trying to apply everything he had been taught, like kicking his legs and flapping his arms, but nothing seemed to work. He lost consciousness and remembered nothing else until he found himself lying on his back on the grass at the side of the pool with what felt like half the school on his chest.

Leonard was the one who had fished him out, and he was the one who kept jumping up and down with David's chest as his trampoline, until he had coughed up all the water he had swallowed. In later years whenever David thought of the incident, he was continually amazed that Leonard had acted on his own initiative, before any of the teachers were even aware of what had happened. He believed that all the boys who stood around watching were far more interested in Leonard's actions than in calling a teacher. By the time one did arrive on the scene, Leonard was a hero.

**a paved or grassy walkway on the side of the road*

"Your thanks to me?" Leonard would shout at him whenever he spoke about the incident, making sure that David would never forget. "You pushed me off you, and then tried to kill me, punching me in the stomach. What did you do that for, hey? What did you do that for?"

David still remembered how tears had streamed from his eyes because his ribs had hurt with every breath and every cough as he coughed more water out of his lungs. He did not remember punching Leonard, and simply accepted Leonard's word that he had. He also did not realise that the incident had cemented a bond between them that would be life-long.

For a number of years afterwards, David would wake up at night with a recurring nightmare of a white wall, with a thin horizontal black line. At one point on that line was a dot, not in the middle of the wall, but a little to the right side. In his dream he always tried to penetrate that wall, to walk through it. It gave a little as he pushed, but it was impossible to break through, and he would wake up in a cold sweat, sometimes screaming. It was only when he was eighteen years old and he remembered the entire drowning episode that the black line snapped one night, and the wall was gone. That was when he realised for the first time how much he truly owed Leonard. At six years old, facing death could almost be called a part of life, and risk-taking, without the fear of its consequences, a part of growing up. At eighteen, however, life becomes more precious, and his appreciation of Leonard's rescue was reflected in penetrating that wall and so subconsciously acknowledging Leonard's action.

Leonard was a hero for that one day. Had his act of heroism occurred today, he most probably would have received a citation from the mayor, but in those days, a pat on the head by a teacher was more than enough.

David became beholden to him, but it was more from his side than from Leonard's side. Being one year older than David, Leonard had placed himself above the situation and conveyed the impression that David was more a nuisance than a friend. Years later, as they sat in the sauna at the gym, Leonard confided in David that he had enjoyed all the attention he had received.

"And you still thanked me by punching me in the stomach," he laughed. "The teacher had to pick you up and shout at you to calm you down." David would nod his head in agreement. The memory was dim and he could only agree with what Leonard told him. Leonard always seemed to remember the scene down to the smallest detail, probably embellishing it as the years passed.

"I saw your black hair floating in the water," Leonard would repeat, "and when I fished you out, I thought you were a goner. I don't know what made me jump on you—instinct probably—but I must have cracked a few of your ribs, because you couldn't laugh without crying for a week."

The smirk on his face would irritate the hell out of David, but he always allowed Leonard his memory. The fuss that was made by everyone, particularly David's parents, probably became the major highlight of his life, although in David's opinion he achieved much, much more when years later the community discovered his true potential.

"You almost killed me," David replied. "Those weeks afterwards were agony, but the worst was when my parents found out. They made me take special lessons until I could swim."

He never ever told Leonard how scared of water he had become and the effort it had taken him to overcome that fear.

"Yup," he would force a smile, "we had a great time."

And so their friendship started, although sometimes, as they grew older, Leonard annoyed David more than he ever knew. David always tried to stand at his side, not that he hero-worshipped him, he simply felt that he was there to protect him against those who would ridicule and tease him; he felt that he owed him for saving his life. David was small for his age and unfortunately rather on the plump side, so that loyalty cost him dearly. For example, there was the time Leonard idolised Jonathan, or Jon-Jon as he was affectionately nicknamed. Jon-Jon was five years older than Leonard and definitely the most popular boy in town. He was good looking, an outstanding athlete, brilliant at school, polite, well-mannered, the type of boy every mother hoped their son would one day become— the type of boy that made David feel sick with envy.

"Why can't you be more like Jon-Jon?" his mother would screech at him whenever he did something she didn't approve of. He was sure that every Jewish mother in Brakenstroom at one time or another scolded their own sons in exactly the same way. This irritated and annoyed him, but what annoyed him even more was when Leonard started making Jon-Jon his role model soon after Jon-Jon's father had died of prostate cancer.

Jon-Jon turned to religion for comfort after his father's death and insisted that everyone call him by his Hebrew name, Yonatan. He started attending synagogue twice a day, dressed in the black frock coat and black felt hat of the orthodox Jew, and encouraged a wispy beard and "peyess" which he curled around his ears. Leonard copied him as far as school regulations requiring "short back and sides" allowed him to.

"Sandler," the prefects at school would threaten, "go and have your hair cut, or else we will take you to Mac."

"But it is part of my religion," Leonard would whine, "I am Jewish," as if that confession would solve his problem.

Mac was Mr. MacDonald the headmaster, who tolerated Jewish customs to the extent that no exams ever fell on any Jewish holidays. He was not going to allow his school discipline to be undermined by religious quirks.

"Cut your hair," David begged Leonard, embarrassed that he was making a fool of himself. He later felt that it was probably because of his constant nagging that Leonard tried to convert him to his new-found fundamentalism, as if to punish him for his lack of religious zeal. He was only just barmitzvah'd, but was forced to attend synagogue every morning before school and every afternoon before six in the evening, simply because Yonatan wanted to observe a year's mourning and Leonard was his faithful disciple. Yonatan needed David to make up the minyan, the ten men needed to commence prayers, and to this day David still remembered how Leonard would wake him at 5:30 every morning by knocking on his bedroom window so that they could be at synagogue in time for the morning service.

"David," Leonard would whisper, prying the window open with cold fingers, "get up, it is time for shul."

David would open one eye and see Leonard standing fully dressed in his school uniform. When he kept the window closed to discourage him, Leonard simply knocked and yelled even louder, waking his parents.

It normally took seconds to dress, but on these days he would slow down, hoping that Leonard would become impatient and run off without him, but Leonard would wait outside, jumping up and down in the cold morning air, slapping his arms loudly around his body to keep warm. Eventually David would grudgingly let himself out of the house and complain bitterly all the way to the synagogue.

"Come on, we're late," Leonard would shout to David as he dawdled, and the two boys would run down the street.

For almost a year, except when Yonatan went on holiday, they both laid tefilin (phylacteries) every morning and prayed twice a day. This was probably one of the reasons David still woke up at 5:30 a.m., but now he went to the gym and not the synagogue. Every morning they kept reciting the same prayer as is the custom with Judaism. At that age, David became convinced that God was tired of hearing the same praises, usually said very fast because they had to finish the service in twenty minutes or less so that they could be at school on time. He often wondered whether He ever really heard them and became convinced that He didn't, because his school marks never improved, even though he prayed religiously every other morning and almost every evening for six months. After that he gave up following the service from the siddur (prayer book) and would stand watching the others pray while he tried to complete his homework.

Today, as an adult, he often thought about these events, and supposed that, in spite of this youthful observation and growing cynicism in his very formative years, he still had a bit of religion, because he did like going to synagogue on a Friday night. He liked the traditions of Judaism. He liked being a Jew. Leonard grew into the type of man who, when you wanted something done, like filling a chairmanship that no one else wanted or the position of secretary within a committee, was always the last choice, but when elected, turned out to be the best choice.

David simply did not believe Audrey when she phoned him at his office in Johannesburg on that fateful Monday morning and said, "I have just heard that Leonard has died."

"You must be mistaken, Audrey," he almost shouted, upset at the possibility that she was right. "Mrs. Sandler, Leonard's mother, was very ill. It must be her."

"Well, whatever," Audrey replied calmly, hurt that David would have considered doubting her. "I just thought you should know."

Audrey still lived in Brakenstroom. Leonard and David had moved their families to Johannesburg years before. The decision to move had not been an easy one; they had followed their children who simply never came home to Brakenstroom after achieving their degrees at the various universities throughout South Africa.

David could understand and accept their decision not to return; over the past thirty-five years Brakenstroom had become a predominantly Afrikaans community with an Afrikaans culture, distinct from the English culture it had once had. David's late father had probably been the last English-speaking mayor and the only Jewish one the town would ever have. King Edward Street, the main street, became Kerk (Church) Street and all the other English names in the town were given Afrikaans names, to the dismay of many. The new and much-hated political ideology of separate development (apartheid) designed by the ruling party to separate the different racial groups separated the different language groups as well. Children from the small Jewish community migrated to the large English-speaking cities and their reluctant parents soon followed them. Leonard and David maintained their friendship in Johannesburg, although they saw a great deal less of each other than they had when they lived in Brakenstroom.

David stood with the phone to his ear listening to Audrey breathing. His thoughts were in disarray. He knew that Audrey was very rarely mistaken in what she said. Although she was not the local gossip, she did somehow manage to know about everyone's affairs, especially those of the Jewish community. He frowned at the thought that Leonard might truly be dead.

"Audrey," he replied after a few minutes, "I'll go to their home right away and ring you from there."

Leonard and Sonja's house was a short distance from David's office. All the way in the car, he kept remembering Leonard's words to him almost a year before. They had sat in the sauna of the gym after a workout, talking about choir rehearsals for Rosh Hashana, when suddenly Leonard's eyes started to wander.

"Well," he had said casually, the sweat dripping off the tip of his nose, his eyes avoiding David's enquiring stare. "Dr. Benjamin says that my ticker is not acting the way it should."

Leonard always liked to drop bombshells like this in the middle of a normal conversation. Without even catching a breath, boom, it was out, and he knew that David would be concerned. David should have realised that Leonard was going to make a major statement. He had a way of pulling his lips into his teeth and pinching the muscles of his nose into what Deidre, David's wife, called a "faygella," which meant a bird. He did this whenever he had something to say that was important, and at the same time his eyes would drift rather than look directly at you, but he was always aware of your every movement, waiting for a reaction.

As David drove, weaving in and out of the traffic, he remembered how Leonard had looked that day in the sauna. He had sat on the hard Oregon pine slats, leaning against the back wall, a towel draped casually over his loins, with his long thin legs stretched out and almost touching the floor. His six feet tall frame was skinny enough so that David could see each and every rib in his chest above the slight pot-belly that had started developing over the last three years. He remembered how Leonard had smiled when he had heard David's sharp intake of breath as he had broke the news and how he had carefully poured more water on the coals, raising new clouds of hot steam, his dank long brown hair falling over his eyes.

"Heart problems?" David remembered thinking. "Only overweight people suffer from heart problems, and Leonard is far from overweight. Why should he have a heart problem?"

"Why did you go to Benjamin?" he had remembered asking him.

"I needed an insurance check-up," Leonard had replied, stretching as though already bored with the topic, yet relishing David's concern.

"What did he say, exactly?" David had tried not to sound overly curious.

"He said that the gout pains across my chest were not gout pains, and that I should be more careful with any exercise that I do."

Leonard's words mocked him. If only he had believed him. His eyes misted and he reduced his speed while he groped for a Kleenex.

He remembered how closely he had studied Leonard's face, looking for *some* sign that he was joking. Leonard's brown eyes had looked back at him soulfully, filled with a longing for the popularity that had avoided him all his life.

"That was when Leonard had smiled," he thought. He had seen the smile and had leaned back against the hot wooden wall of the sauna, a little less anxious, but he still remembered demanding, "Then what the hell are you doing in the sauna? You know your blood pressure will go sky high."

Only then had Leonard looked at him, his eyes searching for something deep inside him. Then he had laughed, shrugged, and changed the subject.

David had forgotten about this conversation until now, and as he drove slightly above the speed limit, he kept hoping that Audrey was wrong. He had last seen Leonard three days before.

"I think I will join your gym," Leonard had told him, "because I miss our talks in the sauna. Johannesburg has one thing that I don't like, and that is the loss of intimacy of a close friendship, the price one must probably pay when one moves to a large city."

A gallery of cars had already parked on the sidewalk of the street where Leonard and Sonja lived. David found parking with difficulty and half walked, half ran up the driveway and into the open front doorway. In the hall, Leonard's mother sat crying into the telephone.

He was shattered.

David found Sonja among the crowd that had come to share her grief and wished her "a long life," as is the custom. She pulled him towards her and hugged him, crying on his shoulder.

"He got out of bed at about three in the morning because he had a bit of indigestion," she sobbed. "When he didn't come back to bed, I went looking for him and found him in the kitchen. His head was on his arms, as though he were sleeping, a bottle of antacid next to him. The doctor said that he had had a massive heart attack."

David comforted her as best he could, but she heard nothing and turned and repeated the story to the next comforter, and probably the next, as though the simple repetition would bring Leonard back to her. Max, David's brother, sat in the corner of the room. He and his wife Esther still lived in Brakenstroom, where he practised medicine. They hugged each other, overcome with the emotion of the afternoon. David looked sombrely at Max. "Do you realise," he said, his voice filled with emotion, "that Leonard has died exactly a year after Maurice was killed?" Maurice, a friend from Brakenstroom, but almost ten years their junior, had died in a light plane crash while flying from Durban, "and that Sam," he continued referring to another friend from Brakenstroom, "drowned three years ago in the same month." David said this as though looking for some supernatural connection. Max nodded, agreeing with him.

Later that afternoon, as David sat on the porch of his house sipping a stiff scotch while Deidre prepared dinner noisily in the kitchen, he thought about Leonard and what his death meant to him.

"My immortality has been destroyed," he thought moodily, looking at the amber liquid in the glass in his hand. He held it up to the sun and absentmindedly squinted through it. "Everything has been spoiled." He took another sip from the glass, enjoying the bite of the alcohol on his tongue.

He knew that they must all die one day. His mother had died painfully of cancer when she was only sixty-six years old, and his father had died when he turned eighty, but they were a different generation. Leonard was the first of his generation to die naturally, and this disturbed him.

By dying he felt that Leonard had taken immortality away from him just as, years before, Yonatan had taken God away from him. He sat feeling miserable and watched as the sun set in the orange blaze of colour so common in Africa. A cloud swept over the sun's dying face, but a ray escaped in a fan of brilliance, a hand waving farewell. He shivered as a cold breeze swept through the trees. The Egyptian goose that had taken the chimney of the house across the road as its evening perch started honking as night fell, and woke him from his reverie.

He had enjoyed the whisky, but by drinking alone he had broken one of his prime rules. Today, however, rules could be broken. Today, for the first time since he was a child floundering in a swimming pool, he felt mortal and it was a terrifying feeling. His protector, for that is what Leonard must have been to him, was gone.

"What happens," he mused, "when as a non-believer you die, and then, *if* you should wake up on the other side and find that there is *someone* there?" This was a question Leonard had put to him many years before when in a conversation he had rejected God. He never gave Leonard an answer then, because he didn't have one, but whether it was the whisky, the goose, or the sunset, he felt that he had the answer now.

"Why, then you are in deep trouble." he thought apprehensively.

He woke from his reverie when the goose, as though agreeing with his thought, gave a loud honk and flapping its large wings like so many firecrackers, launched itself into the air honking belligerently as it flew over him.

He rose from his chair, glass raised in a toast to the goose as it flew into the dying sun.

Deidre called him for supper.

Dasser

1

DAVID ASHER, OR DASSER as everyone nicknamed him, was David's grandfather on his father's side. David had been named after him, which means that he died before David was born. That is the Jewish way, not to name a child after a parent or grandparent while they are still alive.

For as long as David could remember, David Asher was a portrait on the wall of his grandmother's house, stern and forbidding, with black hair offset by a thick black moustache, and deep black eyes staring at the photographer from under thick bushy black eyebrows. His nose was aquiline and his mouth, with maroon-tinted lips, was neither stern nor relaxed, but slightly pursed as though in disapproval of the photographer. The portrait had captured a good-looking man who commanded respect, even when touched up with watercolour to give it a semblance of reality.

Hanging next to it on the wall, in a matching photograph with a matching black frame, was David's grandmother. Her raven-black hair was tied in a bun behind her head, her wasp-thin waist corseted tightly to show her full bust, and her black-beaded dress buttoned to her throat in a heavily beaded choke collar. David could never accept that the grim, forbidding woman in this photograph and the tall white-haired grandmother he so fondly remembered as brimming with love, were one and the same person.

"That is your grandfather," she would say, pointing to the photo of Dasser, her voice thick and husky, her Lithuanian accent becoming more pronounced with emotion. "He was a fine man," and then she would sigh and nod her head. "He would have loved to have seen you, but ach . . . ." Her voice would soften as she trailed off into Yiddish, wiping a tear from her eye.

At this point David would always run up to her and, wrapping both arms around her legs, bury his face in her dress and beg her not to cry. He felt her loss, although he could not see what she saw in that stern, forbidding man. To be truthful, he was a little scared of him, and as he grew older his fear and respect never diminished.

"Ouma," he would say softly into her dress as he hugged her legs, "Ouma, I am here and I love you."

She would pick him up, hug him tightly and smother him with kisses as she walked to her favourite chair, the eau de cologne she always wore, a perfume he associated with her to this day, lingering in the air. Then, with him in her lap, she would tell him all about his grandfather.

He would listen spellbound, because he loved her stories. With his head against her ample bosom and with his mind full of the wonderful stories about Dasser, heaven could not have been more blissful.

"He was so handsome—and so romantic," she would begin softly as though to herself, rocking him slowly up and down as he sat in her arms. "I fell in love with him the minute I saw him. He was a big man and very, very strong. When he asked me to marry him, I couldn't believe it. He could have married any girl in London, in the world even. I was so in love with him I would have followed him anywhere, just like Ruth in the good book . . ." and his eyes would follow hers as she looked at the family bible on the table next to them. Her head would nod, ". . . and I did." She would continue dreamily, "I followed him from London all the way here, to Brakenstroom."

David would look up at her as she paused in her story, and her eyes would be misted over, a tear slowly tracing its way down each wrinkled cheek. She would reach into a pocket and pull out a snow-white handkerchief. Dabbing at each tear with a sniff, she would not say anything for a while, but would sit, rocking him slowly, deeply lost in her day-dreams. He would keep very still, knowing instinctively that if he moved she would be startled and he would not have a story.

"Did I tell you about the time he bought me a 'spider'?" she would ask after a few minutes. He would shake his head, even though he had heard the story a thousand times before.

"One day," she would begin, her eyes misting again, "when I was in the kitchen making supper, Emily called me."

"Missus," she shouted, "come quickly. Master wants you at the front."

"Emily was our maid at the time, a real good-for-nothing, never kept the house clean and always in her room," she would shake her head in disapproval. After a moment's hesitation as though ridding herself of the thought, she would click her tongue and continue. "She sounded so excited that I ran to the front door, and there in the street stood your grandfather, holding a big black horse with a beautiful black 'spider.' I still remember how polished the 'spider' was, because it shone in the sunlight. Its big wheels had silver spokes, which made it very classy. He made me come for a ride straight away, wouldn't even let me put a scarf on, the meshuggener [crazy man]," and she would shake her head and smile to herself, hugging him tighter.

"Can you imagine," she would continue, her eyes shining, "there I was, dressed in my house clothes with my hair flying out from my head, parading up and down King Edward Street for everyone to see. Oh, but he was so proud. This was the first 'spider' in Brakenstroom, and he had to show it off." She would hug David even tighter, as the memory of those happy times warmed her.

Today it would be a story about the 'spider,' tomorrow it would be another story, but always it was about some grand romantic exploit, as though Dasser had felt the need to compensate for bringing a lovely bride to this dusty rustic village of Brakenstroom.

She had come to Brakenstroom before the tall cypress trees had been planted, and before the first roads had been paved. She came before the huge lake on the Brak River had been built, a lake that would one day make Brakenstroom the greenest and most beautiful town in the Transvaal. To a young bride who had lived in London most of her life, the town must have been truly primitive.

When David was older, he realised that many of his grandmother's stories had grown with the telling, so that he was never sure whether she could distinguish the fiction from the fact. He enjoyed her stories as much as she must have enjoyed having her only grandson a very willing audience. By the time David's brother Max was born seven years later, she had already passed on to join her beloved Dasser.

Even to this day, he remembered sitting in her sunny kitchen, warmed by her coal stove, while she baked hamantaschen[1] and cheesecake squares before Purim.

"Our shtetl [village] always baked hamantaschen and cheesecake together," she would tell him. "Some people just don't like the sharp taste of the maun, so they eat the sweet cheesecake instead."

Her maun filling was poppy seed sweetened with honey. He liked to dip his finger into the sticky dark mixture and scoop out a large glob, which quickly found its way into his mouth. He would sit sucking his finger, watching how she knotted the dough like the four corners of a handkerchief as she prepared the cheesecakes. He remembered how she yellowed the cheese with egg yolk, and how the maun beckoned invitingly through a crack in the crust of the steaming hamantaschen as she took them from the oven. It was always a big decision: which would be the most enjoyable? He would test them both for her, often with his stomach bursting, while she waited patiently for his praise.

"Ouma," he would say hesitantly, unable to swallow another mouthful, "this time the hamantaschen is nicer." But she knew him, and she knew that he always preferred the sweetness of the cheese to the bitter sharpness of the poppy seed.

"Try another piece of the cheesecake," she would coax him. "This time I have used Auntie Eva's recipe, and everyone knows that Auntie Eva was the best cheesecake maker in the shtetl."

He would have to refuse, because he simply could not eat another piece. But she would insist, telling him how Dasser, too, had always preferred the hamantaschen. Whenever he told her that this time the cheesecake was better, somehow Dasser had always preferred the cheesecake. It was a game, their game, and he always looked forward to playing it with her.

2

YEARS LATER WHEN David was a teenager looking for his roots as a young Zionist he asked his father where Dasser had come from. His father told him that Dasser had been born in a shtetl in Poland,

---

1 Haman is from the story of Esther. The cookie is made in a three-cornered shaped like the hat Haman wore. It is filled with bitter poppy seed, sweetened with honey, and is usually prepared and eaten during the Jewish festival, Purim.

and like other Jews in Poland, Lithuania, and Russia had chosen to run away rather than serve in the army under the hated Cossacks. Why he chose South Africa to immigrate to and not America like everybody else was a mystery. The family joked that somewhere along the way he must have boarded the wrong ship. It was when David's nephew, Mark, married in London, that they found out that their grandfather was not only running away from the Cossacks, but he was also running away from someone.

On the day of his wedding, Mark received a phone call from a man who asked whether he was a grandson to David Asher from South Africa.

"Yes, I am," Mark replied, mystified by the call.

"Well, then I am your cousin, the son of the daughter your grandfather and the Abandoned One had together."

"The Abandoned One?" Mark was puzzled. "Who is the Abandoned One?"

"You mean you don't know?" the voice sounded incredulous. "The Abandoned One, my grandmother, was your grandfather's first wife. David Asher abandoned her in Poland when he ran away to South Africa."

This was the first time anyone in the family had ever heard of the "Abandoned One." David and Mark later found out that not even their parents knew about her. Mark invited Teddy Greenberg, his new-found cousin, to the wedding. Teddy politely declined, but insisted that Mark contact him when he and his bride returned from their honeymoon. This Mark did, and was invited to a very comfortable home in Berkeley Square—clearly the Greenbergs were very wealthy.

Mark had written to David describing his visit. David reread part of it to Deidre.

Margo [Mark's wife] and I were met at the door by a butler, who ushered us into a magnificent and tastefully furnished sitting room. Heather Greenberg was waiting for us in front of an enormous fire, which warmed the whole room. She was beautifully dressed with a magnificent string of pearls around her neck. She looked as though she had just stepped from the pages of Vogue. *She is a big woman with reddish auburn hair, absolutely full of beans, and within seconds, simply by her warm and enthusiastic greeting, she made us feel quite at home. She spoke the Queen's English as it should be spoken, and Margo took to her immediately, you know how fussy she can be about liking people!*

After a few minutes, Teddy joined us. He had only just come home from work. He is in the shipping business and apparently owns two or three tankers. This type of relative we definitely do need.

I asked him whether he was sure that his David Asher and our Dasser were one and the same person. He showed me a head-and-shoulder photograph. The portrait looked very similar to the one in the black frame hanging on the wall at the old house. He told me that David Asher had run away from a wife in Poland, leaving her with a baby girl. The marriage had been an arranged marriage, probably the reason he had left her. When he did not return after seven years, the Rabbi had given her a "Get" (Jewish divorce). She then left the shtetl to join her married sister in London, and because of that, was lucky enough to escape Auschwitz, where the rest of the family perished. She, her sister, and their two children were the only survivors from a very large family.

Her daughter Leah, Teddy's mother, had married well and the Abandoned One, or Oumi, as they called her, lived with them. She died when she was about eighty-four years old, not that they were ever sure of her true age.

Teddy told us that she never, ever spoke about David Asher, but she once did let slip that he was living in South Africa. When Teddy saw in the local newspaper that a Mark Asher from South Africa was getting married, he felt that he had to find out whether there was any relationship to the David Asher that was his grandfather.

Mark's letter then went into pleasantries about the family in London. David wasn't really surprised. The whole aura of Dasser, the fact that his father hardly ever spoke about him, the stories his grandmother told him—all lent to the mystery.

3

APPROXIMATELY A YEAR AFTER Mark's wedding, David's mother died painfully of cancer. Her suffering affected his father's health, the stress of her hospitalisation weakened his heart. He died a year later of heart failure. It was left to David to sort through all the personal papers, something he did not mind doing because he had always been fascinated with old documents. Over the years he been fortunate enough to find a few rather valuable Africana at various auctions which he had framed, and which now adorned the walls of his study. Because of this interest, he made a point of reading every letter and every document that his father had kept, documents that went back to the turn of the century. He was pleased to find his grandmother's passport, which was numbered 6723. It was a South African passport, issued on the third of April 1935, soon after he was born.

Under the heading, National Status, someone had written:

> *A national of the Union of South Africa and a British subject by marriage, the widow of a British subject by naturalization—Local Certificate Cape of Good Hope dated 29.11.1900.*

Her passport showed that she had been born in Lithuania on the first of April 1870; that she was five foot six inches tall, had dark brown eyes with grey hair, and walked with a limp. Her husband was described as "Deceased," born in Poland in 1860.

David was surprised to learn that she had a limp. He was also intrigued by the description "the widow of a British subject." He had always believed that his grandfather was a South African citizen. His curiousity stimulated, he started looking for his grandfather's passport, but it was not among the papers. He found nothing at all about him, not even his signature on any documents. It was as though Dasser had never existed.

"He must truly have been a black sheep to have walked out of his home lured by the riches of Africa," he said to his wife Deidre one evening as they sat down to supper. "This explanation seems far more romantic than his simply coming to Africa to desert or escape a demanding wife. To desert a child, though, is something I prefer to ignore—it does not quite fit the romantic image that my grandmother had woven around him. I wonder whether she ever knew that he was a bigamist, or a divorcee, to give him the benefit of the doubt."

"I wonder whether your father ever knew the real story," Deidre asked after a moment's thought, "or even your uncle. Perhaps they did, which is why they never ever spoke about him."

They sat in silence, each digesting their own private thoughts. Then Deidre asked, her brows frowning with the question, "I wonder, do you know whether he ever tried to contact anyone in Poland? Would Max know?"

"I remember that after the war my parents kept sending food parcels and clothes to relatives in Israel," David answered. "These parcels were never acknowledged, so they could have gone to anyone. If there were any survivors from the holocaust, they would by now have become part of the melting pot that is Israel. Too many families adopted Israeli names as they tried to forget the horrors of the past. You know, Deidre," David continued after a moments thought, "it is far simpler to say that Dasser landed in Cape Town sometime between 1886 and 1889. I remember that my father once mentioned those dates as dates Dasser may have left the shtetl, and my grandmother's passport shows that she became a South African citizen in 1900. I know that he fought in the Anglo Boer war, and that he went back to London during the war. Allow anything from between ten to twelve years prior to 1900, which would tie in with the years my father told me. I also remember him saying that he hardly knew Dasser because when he was born, and he was the youngest of three, Dasser was an old man. I suppose that Dasser could have made his way to the Transvaal by train if it extended that far, with other gold prospectors. He would have had very little money, and would then have paid his way by doing odd jobs. I wonder what it was that made him settle in Brakenstroom and not go on to Johannesburg. I think I should look for his tombstone and see if that can tell me anything."

"Why the sudden interest?" Deidre asked.

"Well wouldn't *you* be interested to find out more should a skeleton appear in your closet?" David smiled teasingly. "Joking aside, just think, here is a man my grandmother married and absolutely adored. Now it turns out he had a 'past' and a very mysterious one at that. I am curious. I must find out more."

The cemetery lay to the west of the town, literally on the other side of the railway tracks, as were the prison and the new black township. This was the Cape Town to Johannesburg line and was therefore not a single line, but a complexity of track as shunting yards developed over the years to service the local industry. Sections encroached on the privet hedge that formed the boundary between the rows of graves and the busy steam engines shunting their daily cargo. Although he had been to the cemetery several times before as members of the Jewish community had passed away, David had never once thought of looking for Dasser's tombstone. He was surprised when he found it quite easily. It was the largest tombstone in the Jewish section, a rather elaborate monument, with a column holding an open bible standing on a double plinth. Both plinths were of grey marble, while the column was in a fluted, almost crystalline white. The bible was also in grey marble, ornately carved with its open pages slightly curled, the carved Hebrew letters painted silver. David had often seen it, but because it stood in one of the far corners of the cemetery he had never bothered to investigate as to whose grave it was. He wondered why his father and his two uncles should have spent so much money on the stone. Dasser had died in 1931, at the height of the Great Depression. David knew that although he had owned a number of properties on King Edward Street, after his death the family had been forced to sell them as they could not afford the mortgage payments.

"Probably it represents the esteem that they held him in," he thought, as he stood before the grave. "Ironically, had they only kept the property and bought a less elaborate tombstone, they would have been far better off."

The inscription on the plinths showed that Dasser had been born in 1858, not 1860 as shown in his grandmother's passport. It did not give the day or the month of his birth.

"I suppose no one knew when it was," he thought. "Yet surely he would have chosen one day in the year to celebrate?" He walked around the grave looking for a signature or some mark to indicate who supplied the stone. There was no inscription.

With the little he now knew, he calculated that Dasser would have been about twenty-eight years old when he landed in Cape Town. He had been a tailor like his father before him, but was a very powerful man with unusual strength and built like an ox, in total contrast to the striking delicacy of the fine stitching in the suits he had made. He was also an accomplished violinist and had brought his violin with him to South Africa.

David remembered his father telling him that "his hands were so big and the violin so small and delicate, we marvelled that it didn't break, especially when he played a piece from here," and he would thump his chest above his heart. "Then his bow would come down on the strings with such force that occasionally one would snap. It was incredible. I am sorry that he wasn't alive to see you, he would have been pleased to see that his grandson was learning to play his violin." David was six when he had started taking lessons, but he remembered his father's words as though it was yesterday.

He still had the violin. It was one of his most prized possessions, as was Dasser's full-length tailor's mirror that stood in their bedroom. The huge solid brass scissors that Dasser had used to cut the cloth for the suits he had made lay at its base.

"They built an elaborate monument to him," David told Deidre later that evening. "I always knew that he was a popular and well-liked man because as I grew older so many people would approach me and say, mostly in Afrikaans, 'You must be Daaser's grandson.' They called him 'Daaser,' not Dasser. I suppose David Asher in Afrikaans would be pronounced as Daawid Aaser, giving you 'Daaser' for short. Then they would take my hand in theirs and shake it until I felt as though my arm would fall off. They would tell me what a wonderful man he was, and how lucky I was to have had such a fine grandfather."

"Did you find any inkling of what brought him here?" Deidre asked, tucking her legs under her as she sat in her chair, making herself more than comfortable.

"Uh, uh," David shook his head. "Everyone had always assumed that Dasser had heard about the gold fields of the Witwatersrand, even in Poland, and that the lure of instant wealth simply swept him along with the thousands of prospectors that were travelling to South Africa. They all believed that he intended to go to America, where all the other Jews from the shtetl went, but that he had caught the wrong boat—the one to Africa rather than America. This is probably wishful thinking. What I can't understand, though, is that if he wanted to go to the Ridge of the White Waters, which is what the Witwatersrand was called in those days, why did he stop at Brakenstroom? He only had another one hundred miles to travel after going literally half-way across the world." He looked at Deidre. She was as intrigued with the mystery as he was.

"What was it in Brakenstroom that held him?" he continued. "Whatever I remember of my grandmother's stories, she never ever said anything about it. Today, in retrospect, I feel that she must have known. Yet why did she keep it a secret?"

In his agitation he started pacing the room. Deidre watched him closely, allowing him to test and crystallize his thoughts.

"Here was a man," he summarized, "who had travelled across half the world in the pursuit of riches. He had run away from, or been forced to leave the ghettos of eastern Europe. He had even abandoned a wife and child, and had chosen the wilds of Africa rather than heeded the more glamorous call of America. Yet when he was so near to his goal, he stopped and put down his roots. I always assumed that it was because Brakenstroom was an established town, while Johannesburg was still a golden rumour of prospectors." He paused for a moment staring at the wall, then he turned to her, "I mean, think of it," he said, throwing his arms in the air with frustration. "In 1886 Brakenstroom had become the gateway to the new El Dorado, the Witwatersrand. Rather than become a prospector, Dasser may have decided to stay and earn a good living making suits of clothes for those who had struck it rich. I don't believe that would have been enough to have kept him here. There has to be another reason."

Deidre stifled a yawn. It was late. "Come on, come to bed. I am tired. You are talking around in square circles." She stood up and stretched her cramped legs. He followed her after a few minutes.

It was only many years later when they decided to leave Brakenstroom and move to Johannesburg that they found the answers to all their questions.

4

DAVID AND DEIDRE LIVED in a huge old house, with a nest of storerooms in the back yard. They had, through the years, accumulated crates of documents and old photographs inherited from members on both sides of the family. They always intended to examine these boxes, 'tomorrow,' a word that became an escape from what they both knew would be a drudgery. When they decided to leave Brakenstroom, they were forced to examine each and every crate. David took two weeks off work and started sifting through the crates, discovering a number of documents that he added to his collection of Africana. Anything of historical importance that he or Deidre did not want to keep, they donated to the local University. The rest of the papers they destroyed.

Both soon fell into a routine, unpacking and sorting the crates by day, and then spending almost two hours of every evening reading what they had found. This worked well for a while, but as time passed, David found himself increasingly absorbed in what he found, to the point where he was often reading until well after midnight. It was during one of these very late night sessions, after Deirdre had gone to bed, that he discovered Dasser's secret.

"It was all there in front of me," he told Deidre the next morning. "It was carefully hidden in the binder of one of the old accounting books. The khaki linen had been cut from the inside cover of the book, and this photograph had been slipped in between the linen and the cardboard cover."

He gave her the photo. It was an old sepia photo of a young woman. On the back written in faded violet ink were the words: "To my beloved Dasser, with all my love, Minnie."

"Minnie?" Deidre whispered questioningly, then looked up at him as she held the photograph before her. "Did Dasser have a mistress, or did he know her before he met your grandmother?"

"Well . . ." David answered, "I somehow feel that he knew her before he married Ouma. Perhaps she is the reason he never left Brakenstroom."

"Let's see what else we can find," Deidre said enthusiastically. "It looks like you have more than one skeleton in your family closet!"

They spent the day looking through the boxes for more clues about Minnie, but now that they knew what to look for, they looked with a great deal more care.

In an old brown leather wallet, they found a railway ticket of the 'Nederlandsche Zuid—Afrikaansche Spoorweg—Maatschappij' made out in the name of Wilhelmina Verster. The date was 1898, and it was signed in the same handwriting as that on the photograph.

"Was this Minnie?" they asked each other. The name Minnie could be a nickname derived from Wilhelmina.

Then purely by chance they found a beautiful pencil sketch of her by an unknown artist. It was on the back of a drawing of Theodor Herzl, the founder of Zionism. David remembered that the sketch had always hung in the hall of his grandmother's house, facing the front door so that it was the first thing you saw as you entered the house. The black frame of the drawing had been broken with all the packing, and David felt that with a new frame, it would be a beautiful picture for his study. He had removed the sketch carefully, taking care not to cut himself on the broken glass, and as he turned it over, there she was, pencilled on the back of the parchment. They both knew it was Minnie the minute they saw the sketch and, as if to confirm their suspicion, the name Minnie had been pencilled into the base of the pedestal she stood next to.

"My God, but she was beautiful," Deidre whispered softly.

The artist had caught Minnie as no photograph ever could. She was a very beautiful woman, even by today's standards. Her hair had been caught up behind her head with a curl at each ear. Her dress had a high bodice, buttoned with lace at her throat; it flared from a wasp-like waist into an ankle-length skirt. She posed with her hand on the pedestal, a bowl of what could have been flowers faintly pencilled in. The sketch was unfinished.

"Hah," Deidre teased, "you have a very beautiful skeleton in the closet. Your grandfather must have been quite a guy."

They agreed that Deidre would continue to sift through the crates on her own, while David would see if he could find more about Minnie in the town's archives. It wasn't easy to get access to the archives, but fortunately the town clerk was a good friend, and he put in a good word with the chief librarian.

Many of the old documents had yellowed with age and were almost illegible. The greatest source of information came from the library's prized collection of the local newspaper, *The Brakenstroom Herald*, with copies dating back to 1890. From these David gradually pieced the scraps of information he found into what he believed could be a reasonably accurate history of the events at that time.

There was a short article welcoming Mrs. Wilhelmina Verster back to the town and commiserating with her in her loss. The article never mentioned what her loss was.

"She could have been travelling from the Cape to her home in Brakenstroom after some unfortunate death, possibly that of a parent or a husband," David postulated to Deidre, "and it is quite possible that Dasser was on the train with her. They could have fallen in love, he a lonely twenty-eight-year-old, and she a vulnerable and very beautiful woman. One can easily picture their blossoming friendship over the three, perhaps four days it took for them to travel from the Cape."

Deidre looked at him with scepticism. "That is allowing your imagination to run wild," she said cynically. "The next thing you will tell me is that he rescued her from a tribe of lions, and she fell into his arms in undying gratitude." He laughed and shrugged his shoulders.

Minnie Verster

"However," she continued, "I suppose that in the absence of a better story, it will have to do."

"I also found this advert for Dasser's taylor shop," he said, handing her a photo-stat copy he had made. "But I did not find any of her personal papers or any other reference to him. Had it not been for the photo in his passport, the railway ticket in a forgotten wallet, and the pencil sketch, we would never have known anything about her. There must be more. I must simply look more carefully."

Then, after days of searching, and just as he was about to give up, he had a lucky break. One of the black cleaning staff heard him ask the chief librarian if she knew of any records regarding Wilhelmina Verster.

"Aach, my Ouma used to work for her," she interrupted. "Man, even today she keeps calling for her Miss Minnie and talking about her. You would think that she was still alive."

"Your grandmother worked for her?" David asked excitedly. "And she is still alive? Can I meet her?"

"Sure, but you will have to come to my house in the Location," she answered. "She is too old to travel."

They arranged an afternoon suitable for a visit. A white person simply could not travel unescorted into the "Location," as the black township was called. It was too dangerous. David would have to be escorted to her house by a policeman. When he told Deidre about the proposed visit, she was as excited as he was.

"This is incredible," she said. "To think that there is still someone alive that can tell us so much about the past, and especially about your family!"

The new Location, distinct from the old Location, had been planned on two hills in the west of the town, separated from the town by the railway line, shunting yards, and the town's cemetery. Where the old Location had simply mushroomed in the marsh land no one wanted, the new Location had been planned, and sited in such a way as to encourage industry to develop around it. The whole concept was part of the government's separate development plan.

With too little money going into the new Location and under the apartheid ideology, the township soon became a slum as squatters moved in from the surrounding districts. Ironically, the site that been chosen for the Location was on the finest ground in the area, as the residents had a magnificent view of the whole of Brakenstroom beneath them. In winter, when the smoke from the numerous chimneys settled in the valley, causing untold health problems amongst the white elderly, the black residents of the new Location were breathing gloriously clean fresh air.

Emily, Minnie's maid, was in her late nineties, and was permanently bedridden. She lay in her bed in a cramped dark room at the back of the house. It was small, as were all the houses in the township, and sparingly but tastefully furnished. Some of the pieces were antique, the owners probably not realising their true value.

Mary was senile, childlike in her old age. When they questioned her, she would fade in and out of her memories, like a spring-driven gramophone that had to be wound up. Most of her answers echoed their questions, and they were not sure how much she truly remembered and how much they suggested. Nevertheless, with much patience and perseverance, they were able to build a sequence of events that gave them a scrappy picture of Minnie and life in Brakenstroom in the 1890s. Fortunately, Deidre had insisted that they take a tape recorder with them. When they returned home later that evening, they replayed the events of the afternoon over and over again, gradually putting the pieces together.

Mary told them that her 'Miss Minnie' had run a boarding house, and when asked whether she knew anything about Dasser, she looked about the room wildly, then smiled in a toothless grin, covered her mouth with her hand, and giggled.

"That Mr. Dasser," she said in one of her cohereant moments, "he was such a nice man, but oh . . . he was so big, and could he *eat*! Miss Minnie was always saying that he would eat her out of house and home." Then she would fade once more into her memories, while they would try to coax some more coherence from her ramblings.

They persisted, and gradually succeeded in extracting a few more pieces of her story. But suddenly, as though angry at their prying, she shouted, "Ag, man, my Miss Minnie, she loved him," Then she said coyly, almost in a whisper, "He was Miss Minnie's skelm' [secret lover]." She giggled, her eyes lighting up her face, then the spark died as she slipped once more into her dreams.

From the scraps she had given them, they worked out that Dasser was one of three boarders that Minnie catered for. He had lived in her house from 1888 until Minnie died in 1899. David remembered reading that Brakenstroom had suffered a diphtheria epidemic at that time and they suspected that Minnie could have been one of its victims.

"She may have contracted the disease, although it is unusual for an adult to become infected." David speculated. "Apparently the epidemic had killed a large number of children in the town. I think that I must try to find her grave. It would be in the Christian part of the cemetery and I have never been there. It could tell us something."

The next day, while Deidre was busy with the last box of papers and breathing a sigh of relief that the end was in sight, David drove the two kilometres out of town to the old cemetery.

"Why is it," he asked himself, "that cemeteries should be framed with pointed cypress trees?" This one was no exception, but a few of the trees were starting to die, a date stamp as to their age. He parked outside the cemetery's huge wrought iron gates, a legacy of the part played by Brakenstroom in the Anglo-Boer War. They had been cast from the cannon that the British Army had captured from the Boers and displayed heroic scenes from the siege of Brakenstroom. A large number of the British dead were buried in neat rows in one corner of the cemetery, while the Boer dead had been buried on their family farms. He remembered reading about the gates in one of the old travelogues. In those days they were one of the features of the town. He wondered how many people knew about them today.

He walked among the tombstones, most of them cut of white marble, but rotting in their neglect with the invasion of moss and small plants that had taken root in the tiniest cracks. Some of them were elaborate monuments depicting the sculptor's image of the after-life, while others were simple slabs with the engraved words showing remnants of black or gold paint. The sandy paths between the rows of graves had been kept free of weeds, but the individual care of the tombstones had been taken over by the elements.

David gradually worked his way toward the earliest graves by following the dates inscribed in the plinths of each tombstone, and without too much difficulty found Minnie's grave. Emily had been right in saying that Minnie had died in 1899.

The inscription on her tombstone had been almost obliterated by the red sand that had accumulated in the carved words. Her grave was in one of the front rows under a tall cypress tree, and was guarded by a small angel carved out of white marble. Years of neglect had given moss and grass a hold in seams of the stone drapery, and the marble looked veined as the hot sun of the day and the cold frost of a winter's night had created a myriad of tiny cracks over the years. One of the angel's wings had broken off and lay on the ground.

David stood looking at the grave. He was filled with emotion. It seemed so strange to him that the woman who lay there had played such a large part in his destiny. He broke a twig off the privet hedge that invaded the cemetery in this desolate corner and carefully scratched the sand out from the inscription. He read:

"My beloved Minnie, who gave me such happiness."
M.H.S.R.I.P.
WILHELMINA ANNA VERSTER
1869–1899

There was no indication as to who the mourner was.

He sat on his haunches, his chin in his hand, thinking about this woman of the past, a woman whom he knew only from a sketch and the odd scraps of memory he had gleaned from a faithful and loving maid. He wondered whether she was indeed his grandfather's paramour.

"She must have been a remarkable woman, if she was," he thought, "in that she had stolen him from a family he had in Poland, and had stopped him from travelling to the golden city of Johannesburg that he had travelled so far to find. I wonder whether Dasser visited the grave while he was married to my grandmother?" he reflected as he looked around for some sign to show that he had. But he saw nothing; not even a vase with dead flowers. The grave looked no different from any of the others except for the small broken angel guarding it. He read the inscription again. Something about the wording bothered him, but he could not put his finger on it.

He stood up, dusting the sand from his trousers, idly looking around at the other graves to see if they were in worse or better condition than hers. Suddenly, three graves away, he noticed a grave guarded by an angel that was identical to hers but smaller, its face turned toward her grave. One side of the plinth had collapsed, pushed over by the root of the privet bush that formed part of the hedge. The similarity of the two angels struck him as unusual. He walked to the grave and carefully wiped away the sand from the inscription. The year was the same, the dates a few days apart. The inscription read:

"Cecil, my son, watch over your Mother"
"M.H.S.R.I.P"

Then he realised what it was that had bothered him about the inscription on Minnie's tombstone. The letters M.H.S.R.I.P. were more commonly found on a Jewish tombstone. Christians usually inscribe "R.I.P.", meaning "Rest in Peace", whereas "M.H.S.R.I.P." means "May His/Her Soul Rest in Peace."

"My God," he thought in amazement, "Dasser and Minnie had a son and this is his grave. He must have been one of the victims of the diphtheria epidemic, probably infecting his mother as she nursed him."

He quickly cleaned more of the tombstone, working away the sand that had built up over the years. The name of the child that lay there gradually revealed itself.

CECIL VERSTER
1893–1899

There was now no doubt in his mind that Cecil must have been Dasser's son. Both tombstones were in English, and both had a similar appearance. The fact that the child's name was Verster meant that they were not married. He started speculating as to how Minnie had been able to have an illegitimate child without creating a scandal. She may have simply done what most unmarried mothers in Brakenstroom probably did, which was to move to another town for a few months, and then come home with a "sister's" child, a sister that had too large a family and did not want the extra mouth to feed.

"Some people may have speculated that the child could be Dasser's," he thought, looking at the grave. "Would either of them have wanted that? But then again, the inscription reads 'Cecil, my son.' Did Dasser decide to acknowledge him as his son only after he had died? It is something I will never know."

The double tragedy must have been a great blow. David remembered his father telling him that it was his mother who had kept all the Jewish traditions in the family and insisted on keeping the kosher laws in their home. Dasser was a non-practising Jew.

He sat for a long time at the two graves, thinking about Cecil, the boy that never was. He had come into this life quietly, almost secretly, and had left it just as quietly, never to be remembered, other than by a tombstone on a forgotten grave.

A crow screamed and woke him from his reverie. He looked up and watched the sun turn to into a huge orange red ball as it sank below the cypress trees. He shivered as a cold breeze wafted over the cemetery. The sun, like a watchful parent, fingered each and every tombstone as it sank below the horizon. He stood up, stretched his cramped muscles and, after placing a small stone on each grave, he went home.

5
DASSER'S STORY

THE BIBLE TALKS OF THE LAND of Canaan as being the land of milk and honey, but to the Voortrekkers who trekked north from the Cape to escape British domination, the Highveld of the Transvaal was the promised land, and so it was, with its incredible reservoir of gold. They did not know this when they settled in their new home. They only saw the richness of the soil and the beautiful grasslands called "veldt" stretching to the horizon. The high altitude, four thousand feet above sea level, gave them a cool, wonderful climate with endless days of beautiful blue sky studded with cumulus clouds that stepped upwards into the heavens. Their paradise was framed by gently swelling hills and criss-crossed by countless streams and rivers that fed the mighty Vaal River in the South and the Crocodile River in the north.

They had trekked in wagons drawn by oxen over unknown terrain, until hundreds of miles lay between them and the hated British. As they migrated, they fought numerous bands of marauding natives, who regarded their vast herds of cattle as common property. The land was empty, with no rightful owner, and with a rifle in one hand and a bible in the other, they laid their claims, establishing their farms on the rich veldt.

Eventually two Boer Republics were founded, one in the Transvaal and the other in the Orange Free State. This was a declaration of their independence as they looked for obscurity, where they could live their lives and practise their religion away from the world's eye. This was not to be. Diamonds were first discovered in the Free State at Kimberley, and then gold on the Witwatersrand of the Transvaal. Speculators from all over the world soon flocked to the two republics, much to the consternation of the conservative Boers. Their isolation was shattered. The British Empire was on their border and Cecil John Rhodes was building his financial empire.

When the Anglo-Boer War broke out in October of 1899, Dasser fought for the Boers because he had always considered himself to be a Boer. The war was a godsend to him. He had suffered tremendous tragedy and here was a means to forget. He felt that God had punished him because he had deserted a family in Poland. He therefore rejected God. The suicidal recklessness he displayed was tantamount to a death wish. He had lost a dear one and above all he had lost a son.

At thirty-seven years old, he had become a fine horseman and a good shot, having in happier times spent many a day hunting game with his Boer friends. Unfortunately for him, very early on in the war he collected a bullet in his right lung and very nearly died. With his strong constitution and in spite of his desire to join his beloved Minnie and their son, he lived, but before he could go to war again, he was given a special assignment.

His heroism had earned him the respect of President Paul Kruger, who had, in more peaceful times, been one of his regular customers. Dasser had made innumerable suits for him and had visited Pretoria a number of times as his guest.

Because of the war, the Republic could no longer buy sugar from the plantations of Natal. Oom Paul, as President Kruger was called by all, turned to Dasser for assistance and asked him to lead an expedition to the port of Lorenzo Marques in Mozambique. This port was the Transvaal's only access to the sea at that time, and the ride through the lowveld would be a long and dangerous one.

The lowveld of the eastern Transvaal differs from the open grass plains of the Transvaal highveld, in that it is true bushveld, the home of the big game. It is also the home of the malaria mosquito and the dreaded Tsetse fly that causes sleeping sickness. Daily doses of quinine made blood bitter and so prevented the mosquito from drawing blood and passing on the malarial parasite. There was no such deterrent for the Tsetse fly. Dasser knew this. He also knew that the only time of the year that man would venture into the lowveld was during the winter months, from May to October, when the cool night air banished both insects.

The red blooms of the Kaffirboom tree were nature's signal that summer was near and also a sign that the lowveld was a dangerous place to be in. Dasser agreed to go—not that he had any option, as he was still officially in the Boer Army.

While most miners and prospectors left the lowveld to the herds of game, travelling up the escarpment back to the cooler, almost treeless Highveld, he and the two riders who made up his party descended into the sweltering heat of the lowveld.

The journey through the long grass and the dense bush sapped his strength. He had not fully recovered from his wound. One of the men died painfully of sleeping sickness and was buried on the banks of the Crocodile River. The other contracted tick-bite fever and had to be nursed through bouts of extreme illness. Dasser, still taking the dreadful-tasting tonic his doctor had given him earlier to help him recuperate from his wound, started to believe that the chemicals circulating in his blood kept the insects away, because not even a flea bit him. When they eventually arrived in Lorenzo Marques, he was exhausted in spite of the tonic, but he fulfilled his task and then rested.

He decided not to return to the Transvaal until he had recovered completely. It was also mid-summer, and to travel back through the bush of the lowveld would now be more than foolhardy. After a short rest, he boarded a ship bound for Durban, with the intention of making his way back to Brakenstroom via a less trying route. Unfortunately, because of his Boer passport he was not allowed to disembark and had to continue on to Cape Town. Once again, he was not allowed to disembark and was told that if he did so he would be arrested as a Boer spy. The ship was sailing to England and so, very much against his will, he sailed with her. He needed the rest, and the sea air soon restored him back to good health. His recent tragedy became a dim, distant memory.

6

"YOUR GRANDFATHER," Ouma would tell David years later, "nearly became a spy. The British wanted to put him in gaol, and oy vay, if they had, then he would never have come to London and we would never have been married. Always remember that he was a brave man and that he fought like a mensch [a shrewd and clever man.]"

"When I saw him for the first time in London," she would continue, "he was so handsome. His skin was brown, like chocolate, and with his full black beard and the wonderful stories he told, he was so popular. At all the parties, the girls would sit around him and look at him as though he were a great Jewish hero. He looked just like that picture of Theodor Herzl in the hall. The men would stand around, a little jealous, but then Dasser was such a wonderful man. He never made any enemies. Everybody loved him."

The way she spoke about Dasser boosted her ego for having caught and married him even though he was much older than she was. She was an immigrant from Lithuania and had only just lost her husband to the influenza epidemic. Her married name was Kutchinsky, and she was still in mourning when Dasser came into her life. They must have waited the year's customary mourning period before they married, because their wedding certificate showed that they married thirteen months after she had buried her husband. She had a daughter, Ruth, who was three years old and is the flower girl in their wedding photo, which hangs in David's study with all the other Africana.

It was probably during this time that Dasser had met Meish, a man far younger than he. They were to become lifelong friends. Meish is best man in the wedding photo, standing just behind Ruth.

On the sixteenth of January 1902, they must have arrived back in the Cape, because Dasser applied for letters of naturalization from the Colonial Secretary at his offices in Cape Town, Cape of Good Hope. They were granted, to a Mr. and Mrs. D. Asher, of 68 Caledon Street, Cape Town.

Dasser's papers now showed that he was a British citizen, probably due to his marriage. He and his new wife and daughter took a train to Brakenstroom, but they were stopped at the town of Parys on the Vaal River and not allowed to enter the Republic, as the Anglo-Boer War was still being fought. He used his Boer passport to visit Pretoria, so that he could obtain permission from Paul Kruger for his wife and daughter to enter the Transvaal. Of course permission was granted, but probably not by Oom Paul, as he may have been in Switzerland by then—unless it was one of his last acts before he had fled his country in a vain attempt to raise the much needed capital for the ailing Republic.

On the thirty-first May 1902, the Anglo-Boer War came to an end, with a treaty drawn up in Vereeniging and signed in Pretoria. Why Dasser ever returned to Brakenstroom, a town where he had suffered such tragedy, is a mystery. And why he should bring a new wife to a town that knew of his previous "life" is even more of a mystery. David could only guess that it was because he had numerous properties and assets. He must have told her about his past—perhaps when they were still in London—because if he hadn't, she would most certainly have found out. Documents do show that soon after arriving in Brakenstroom, he purchased another property and built a house for his new bride, where they had three sons.

When he died in 1934 he was seventy-two years old and, although there were no photographs of him as an old man, David's grandmother always spoke of him as a man with incredible strength and enthusiasm for life. She died when David was seven years old. It was a dark dreary day, with the typical summer thunderstorm crossing the veldt. He remembered vividly how, after coming home from school, he went to her house as he normally did, but was met at the gate by his mother and taken home. He remembered his parents talking in whispers and looking sad and eventually, after a week, when he did go to her house to look for her, she was not there.

For years after, he played in the old house. Her one bachelor son, Max, lived there alone. David often spoke to her ghost and rediscovered secrets they had shared and enjoyed. When the house was sold after Max married, he kept the two portraits of Dasser and Ouma. They hang on the wall in his home to this day. Deidre often begs him to throw them away, as they are very gloomy formal portraits, but he simply cannot.

Next to the two pictures, on the wall, is a portrait of Theodor Herzl, beautifully drawn in pencil. Both the front and back are glassed. Every so often he turns the portrait around to look at Minnie, and when he does he is convinced that a slight frown forms on the forehead of his grandmother. Feeling guilty, he quickly turns Minnie's face back to the wall.

It keeps the peace.

Meish

1

AT THE END OF THE Second World War, the Nationalist Party under Dr. D.F. Malan came to power and, for the first time since the Anglo-Boer War, Afrikaner nationalism controlled South Africa's destiny. The residents that made up the town of Brakenstroom were, under the new government, not only divided along racial lines (as was common in all South African towns and cities), but were now further divided into those who spoke Afrikaans at home, and those who spoke English. Afrikaans schools were only for white-Afrikaans speaking children, while English schools were for everybody else, excluding anybody with colour who in turn were classified as Coloureds (people of mixed blood), Indians, and "Natives," as the blacks were called. Japanese and Chinese presented a problem because South Africa needed trading partners as her isolation grew. First the Japanese and later the Chinese, because of trade with Taiwan, were declassified, and became "White." All these "separate developments," a phrase used by politicians to ease their consciences—were legislated, becoming notorious throughout the world as the South African apartheid (separate development was the nice name, apart hate was the true name) system.

Like any ordinary town, Brakenstroom had the very rich, the very poor, and all those in between. Two social groups, however, stood out above all the others: the professors and lecturers of the local university, and the Jewish community. To be associated with the university and own a Mercedes Benz motor car was the height of snob appeal; while to be a Jew gave one access to all of the different social and racial groups, although this did not guarantee acceptance by any of them. Anti-Semitism *did* exist in Brakenstroom, especially among the Afrikaner elite, and every Jew was constantly aware of it and knew that receiving any business from the University was not to be, as it openly supported only Afrikaner concerns. This unwritten law was a constant source of irritation to anyone that was not an Afrikaner.

The town also had its share of characters, but none was more eccentric, better known and accepted by all the various population groups than Meish Leibowitz. Everybody knew him, and everybody could tell you a story that somehow involved Meish, a story that made you chuckle when you heard it.

Meish gave one the impression of being simple, always laughing and always dressed as though he never had a cent to his name. But in a game of poker (when one could persuade him to play), or in a game of bridge (which he loved to play), he was cold and calculating, taking only as much money from you as he felt he needed at that moment.

He was tall and rather bony, with a long face framed by thinning grey hair. Most days he never shaved, and on those few days that he did, his face would be covered with bits of toilet paper placed on the razor nicks, as he tried to encourage the blood to clot. His eyes were crinkled from laughter and his nose resembled a twisted ski jump, the result of a fist fight some time in his past.

Meish had been Dasser's best friend, although almost thirty years younger. Dasser had, in a way, been responsible for bringing him from Poland to South Africa, and had always treated him more like a son than a friend. He remained a frequent visitor to the Asher home after Dasser had died, and David could remember his mother always referring to him as "Poor Meish," something he never totally understood, as Meish was not poor, he was simply "not quite there." It was only years later, after David heard Meish's story from his own lips, that he realised that his mother was sorry for him.

Like most eccentrics, Meish had a number of stories attributed to him. Many were true, but many grew and were embellished with the telling as the years passed. The university and its elite were the butt of his humour and made him many enemies, but because he appeared simple, he was mostly ignored. However, he did overstep the mark when, on a very hot day, he offered the then Mayoress of the town a lift home in a Mercedes coupe that was parked in front of his fruit shop. She had been walking home for some reason or other, and was grateful at the offer. He then left her melting in the hot sun for almost thirty minutes, with the excuse that he was going to fetch the keys to the car. When, perspiring profusely, she escaped to the cool shade of the shop, she found that not only did Meish not own a Mercedes, but that he had left by the back door.

Professor Gert Haasbroek, the Mayor, never forgave Meish for ridiculing his wife, but the English speaking community laughed with Meish, and applauded him. When Meish did, one day, buy a second-hand Mercedes, he tore the emblem from the bonnet and trained his cocker spaniel to sit on the hood while he drove through the town. The sight of the dog with its ears flapping in the wind brought the wrath of the SPCA down on him, but he had made his point and 'Mercedes' lost a little bit of its prestige.

Meish never seemed to age or lose his sense of mischief. At any party, he quickly became its life and soul until he drank too much whisky, when someone would have to drive him home. When eventually he did age, he became old very, very quickly. To David he was simply always there, and it was only when he and Deidre spent a week holidaying in Muizenberg that David got to know more about his life, and how he had come to South Africa. Gertrude, Meish's daughter, invited David and Deidre to share a flat with them in Muizenberg. She had recently lost her husband in a tragic accident and had brought Meish with her for a short holiday. It became David's duty to walk with Meish on the beach at six o'clock every morning. By then Meish was close to ninety years old and a one-kilometre walk took almost two hours, because every so often he would have to stop to let his angina pains pass.

"And those idiot doctors told me that one whisky a day would keep my blood pressure down," he would grumble in his thick Yiddish accent, as though blaming them for his heart problem. "Whisky is the only thing that keeps me alive—it's like mother's milk," and he would mumble to himself, cursing every doctor that he had ever met.

"It is quite remarkable," David told Deidre the first evening, "that although in growing up, I have seen Meish for almost twenty years and laughed with everybody else at all his stories, I have never ever said more than a 'Good Morning Mr. Leibowitz,' to him. I do remember my father telling me that in his youth Meish had been a dynamic personality with an incredible sense of humour. Somehow, my father's description of a younger Meish does not quiet gel with the Meish that we all know. It is as though there are two different people with two different personalities—a young Meish and an old Meish, with the old Meish being slightly off the rails. When he speaks about his life, he is reliving the past and I am beginning to understand what has happened to him."

Over the next two weeks during their walks, David learned more and more about Meish's past life. He found in Meish a tragic man that had first lost someone he had dearly loved and then had found her only to lose her again. This is what had broken him.

2

MEISH WAS BORN IN A shtetl in Poland, close to the Russian border. Because he was the youngest of three sons, he had to serve in the army as soon as he turned eighteen. The eldest son in every family was exempt. Jews in Russia were hated and in the Russian army they became slaves to the Cossacks, who treated them with exceptional cruelty. To escape the army, he did what every Jewish boy tried to do: he simply changed his name so that the conscription officers couldn't find him. He conveniently became the son of Mrs. Leibowitz, a widow in the shtetl who did not have any children. He was 'barmitzvahd' with her surname, and promptly forgot his own, never to remember it again. Being an only child, he was now exempt from serving in the army.

When his adopted mother died, Meish knew that he would have to leave the shtetl for America. His real parents had left many years before, but as time passed they became distant memories to the young man. Because of the lack of urgency, and more importantly, because of Chana, he kept delaying his departure.

Meish had known Chana almost from the day she was born. He and his family had lived next door to the Hershowitz family, and as a young boy he had often had to watch over the new baby whenever the parents visited each other.

"She was the most beautiful baby in the shtetl," he whispered in his Yiddish accent as he and David walked along the beach, the waves frothing up to wet their feet.

"She was a beautiful baby," he repeated, "and she grew up into a beautiful girl. Her mother let her black hair grow long, and she would let it fall around her shoulders and down her back so that it reached here," and he would touch his buttocks. "Her skin was so . . . so white like . . . like . . ." he struggled for a simile, then unable to think of one, he stopped talking as though the emotion of the memory was too much for him.

"That cosmetic firm, Revlon," he would continue as he regained his composure, "if they had only seen her, they would have needed no other girl for their pictures. She was so . . ." and his voice would fade wistfully once more into his memories.

On other days he told David how "Her black eyes had stolen many a man's heart while she was still a child." Suitors continually beat a path to her door, begging her father for a betrothal, as was the custom, but she refused them all in spite of her parents' insistence. She had eyes only for Meish, who was a very presentable young man, tall and good-looking with a beautiful singing voice that echoed through the synagogue when he sang on High Holy days. Everyone in the shtetl knew that he and Chana would be married some day, but that they would have to wait until she was old enough. Only then could he ask her parents, neither of whom approved of her seeing him, for permission to marry her. His adopted mother could not arrange a betrothal for him. She had no money of her own; he supported her with the little money his parents sent him from America and whatever he was paid when he sang in shul.

"He has no money," her mother would shout at her whenever she saw them together. "How do you think he is going to keep you, with his voice? No matter how good he davins (prays) and how beautiful he sings, Cantors, in the shul, you can buy anywhere. Why wait for him?"

But Chana was adamant. She was headstrong, as most favoured daughters usually are, and she knew how to twist her father around her little finger. Her two sisters were already married and had faithfully produced two fine grandsons for their doting grandparents. It was now her turn.

"I love Meish," she would tell her father firmly, as she held his hand in hers. "I have always loved him, and I will marry him as soon as I am old enough. You will give me to him just like you gave my sisters away," and then she would kiss him gently on the forehead, closing all further arguments. He would sigh, shaking his head. Putting both of his arms around her, he would draw her to him, kissing her on her cheek, his grey beard tickling her nose.

Yet every night as he lay in his bed next to his wife, he prayed to the Almighty to show him the way.

Meish was twenty-one when his adopted mother died. Now he had no reason to stay in the shtetl. His birth parents often wrote from America begging him to join them, but he could not leave Chana. She would look at him, her eyes misting, and say, "Meish, you must go, there is no life for you here. You will be taken into the army if you stay. Go now, and send for me in three years time. I will be eighteen then. If you make enough money in America, then Papa cannot say no."

He would kiss away the tears from the corners of her eyes, those that escaped his lips gently tracing a path down her milky white cheeks. He would promise her the world, telling her that three years was too long to wait. He would work hard and send for her far sooner, or better yet, he would simply take her with him. They would elope.

"I can't live without you," he would say, and they would sit next to each other, their hands clasped tightly together, hidden in the folds of her dress, and dream about their future life in America.

Meish was now technically an "orphan." This meant that he had to do service in the army, but he kept avoiding reporting for duty because he wanted to be with Chana. One night he was nearly caught in a Cossack raid as they conducted a house-to-house search for men and boys who had evaded the draft. He had escaped the search by hiding in the water barrel that collected the rainwater from the roof of the house. The water was cold, and grew colder as time passed. Fortunately the captain of the raiding party accepted the bribes without the usual haggling and the horsemen left without the usual unpleasantness. Meish made his way shivering uncontrollably through the dark towards Chana's house, thanking the Almighty between chattering teeth for sparing him from freezing to death in the cold water. Her parents warmed him in front of a roaring fire and fed him passover wine to raise his body temperature.

"You must go—as soon as you can," Chana whispered to him as they sat in front of the fire. He wore one of her father's shirts while his clothes dried, his thin legs stretched out before him, blue from the cold.

"One of these days they will catch you, and then I will lose you forever." Jews in the Cossack army were treated more like slaves than soldiers. The hatred that existed between Cossack and Jew went back to the days, more than a few centuries past, when the Jews were invited to settle in Russia to restore the economy of the country. They were the traders and the moneylenders, envied and later hated by both the nobility and the peasantry.

Meish sat with his head down, shoulders hunched around his ears, drawing the heat of the fire into his shivering body. He leaned towards her and she took him into her arms like a child.

"Meish," she whispered, "you have to go tonight, before I change my mind."

He could hear her heart beating in his ear where his head rested on her chest. He could feel her soft breast with his cheek, her nipple hardening against it. Hesitantly he cupped her breast in his hand and she placed her hand over his, pressing him firmly to her. He felt her tears drip on his cheek and as they found their way to the corner of his mouth, he tasted their salt and it seemed to give him strength. He shuddered and she held him even tighter. They sat until the fire had burned to an ember. He may have slept, he couldn't remember, but he did remember that her dress, where his head had lain, was wet with her tears and he could feel her as though she was naked.

She helped him gather his pitiful belongings together in a small cardboard suitcase and as the sun rose in the morning sky she sent him to America.

"God go with you, my love," she had whispered to him, her voice trembling. "Come and fetch me as quickly as you can. I will wait for you."

He remembered how she had stood on her toes and kissed him softly on the corner of his mouth. As he put his arms around her waist to hold her close, she slipped away and ran to the house, her long black hair streaming out behind her as she ran, catching the golden glow of the rising sun.

Chana's father gave a quick prayer of thanks to the most Holy of Holies for delivering his beloved daughter from this good-for-nothing young man, and immediately started planning to whom she would be betrothed.

Meish cried when he told David how he had walked down the road, his feet more leaden with every step he took away from her. He had nearly turned back, but in the end continued to the next village, where the railway station was. His destination was America, where all good Russian Jews went. He already had his "quota," as the immigration permit to enter America was called; his parents had sent it to him the minute they heard that old Mrs. Leibowitz had passed on, but somehow his plans went awry, because he ended up in South Africa. The reason for this change of plan was Dasser.

Meish and Dasser met, he never said where, but it could only have been in London, in that period of Dasser's life when he had returned to Europe during the Anglo-Boer war. In spite of their age difference, a lifelong friendship developed.

David tried to find out more about their first meeting from Meish as they walked along the beach. He wanted to learn more about his grandfather, Dasser, but all Meish would say was, "Nu, ve met, und ve became friends. Vere ve met I can't remember, but I tink it vas London."

His accent always become worse when he was angry, so David knew not to press too much. He was led to believe that the well-off Jewish Boer and the younger Russian boy must have taken part in some escapade best forgotten. From what he learned from Meish on further walks, they could easily have been involved in more than just an 'escapade,' and his reticence in explaining further was an attempt to keep the dignity of his grandfather unsullied in his mind. Only much later did David learn that in order to earn money to pay for the boat ticket to America, Meish had found work singing in a brothel. It was quite possible that this is where the two men may have met.

That Meish was best man at Dasser's wedding in London was confirmed in the photo of the wedding. That he travelled back to South Africa with the newly married couple was evident from the documents David found when he and Deidre had emptied the crates in Brakenstroom. What he did not know and only learned on their Muizenberg walks was that, whereas Dasser went back to Brakenstroom, Meish continued on to Johannesburg to try and make his fortune.

3

WHEN MEISH ARRIVED IN Johannesburg, he joined a group of prospectors, dazzled by their stories of tremendous wealth that lay beneath their feet. Like all the fortune hunters of that day, he felt that the road to quick riches lay in finding a payable reef, a vein of gold in the hard granite that threaded through the rock. He struggled more than anyone else, because what did a young Russian Jewish boy know about mining? He had to learn the hard way, so he slaved with the workers on the gold fields, digging in the tunnels, learning how to crush rock and how to extract that elusive yellow metal. Whenever he could, he would visit his older friend in Brakenstroom and accept with great protestation, a gift to help him survive the harsh life of a miner, a gift he was always grateful to receive.

During the days, while he worked, he forgot about his beautiful Chana. But in the evenings, when he rested, he would lie on his bed and before passing out from exhaustion, he would think about her, his heart aching with loneliness.

"I always dreamed about her with her hair flying out behind her as she ran from me," he said as he poked at a jelly-fish lying in the wet sand. "In my dream I would try to see her face, but when she turned to look at me, she was always crying. I would wake up with my heart painful in my chest, here," and he thumped his thin chest with the handle of his cane, "and then I would look up at the dark ceiling of my room and pray to the Almighty, asking Him to make her laugh and smile."

Meish worked hard, some nights collapsing on his bed too tired to eat. He saved his meagre wages carefully, because he wanted his own business. Above all, he wanted to be a man respected in the Jewish community of Johannesburg. He kept his eyes open and looked and waited for an opportunity. Hard work and an agile brain soon took him above ground, earning him more money and allowing him to become that degree more respectable.

Being a good devoted Jew, he tried to remain faithful to his religion, always attending Friday night prayers. With his beautiful singing voice echoing through the synagogue as he joined the congregation in prayer, all the congregants soon knew him. He was often invited to a Friday night meal, usually to those houses that boasted a marriageable daughter, but he remained devoted to his lovely Chana. No one could take her place in his heart.

"It was a way to eat," he smiled. "There were all these girls, big ones, small ones, thin ones, and fat ones. I remember one very fat one. Oy vay, and was she fat," and he shook his head at the thought, "but she was the best out of all of them. If I wanted to marry, she is the one I would have chosen."

"The food they gave me to eat was wonderful. Often it was the only good meal I would eat the whole week. They always told me how their daughter made this, or baked that," and he would chuckle, and look at David slyly out of the corner of his eye, "but I knew it was Mama's cooking. They couldn't fool me. Some of the girls were pretty, but none were as beautiful as my Chana." He paused, thinking to himself.

"I suppose I should have told their fathers that I was more interested in Mama's cooking than in Mama's daughters," and he continued wistfully, "but when you are hungry, and especially when you are lonely, you will do a lot of things that you regret later on in life."

One Saturday morning, after the synagogue service, a wealthy Johannesburg merchant approached Meish.

"It was just what I was waiting for," Meish said, stopping and looking at David. "Being nice to all those girls paid off. Mr. Greenblatt's daughter was perhaps one of the prettier girls. I can't remember what she looked like, but he offered me this job, perhaps to make me acceptable as future mishboggah [family]. He asked me to manage one of his shops. He was also from Russia. You remember him, XYZ Stores."

XYZ stores was a group of stores that was started in Johannesburg at the turn of the century. Over the years, it grew into a large chain found in most South African towns. The company had eventually been absorbed into one of the conglomerates during the 1967 stock market boom.

"He asked me to open a branch for him in Koster," Meish continued, "because he felt that Koster would become the next farming centre in the Transvaal. A lot of Jewish families had moved there. I think he had a cousin there."

He had stopped walking when he told David this. Something in his memories had brought on the angina pains. He carefully took his bottle of Glyceryl Trinitrate pills from his pocket, placing one under his tongue. After a few minutes the pains passed.

"I think we should go back to the flat," David suggested, horrified at the thought that Meish could drop dead even while they spoke.

"No . . . no . . ." Meish said with a grimace. "I get the pains often. They soon go away."

The sun was rising in the sky and it was becoming hot. David took his arm to help him, but he shook him off.

"I am not that old, or that sick," he chuckled. "Leave me, I will tell you when I need you." Then he continued with his story.

"I didn't even know where Koster was," he said as though nothing had happened, "but I went. I had never, ever in my life sold anything to anybody, but I knew that this was what I was waiting for."

He was determined to succeed and, above all, he was enthusiastic. He arrived in Koster bright-eyed and ready to tackle the world barehanded, if need be. This was the opportunity that he had come to South Africa for and he was determined to make enough money to send for Chana.

The company had previously found premises for their store in Koster, and he was disappointed to see that it was empty, without any fixtures or fittings, let alone stock. He had been given a certain amount of capital to employ local artisans to build the store's fixtures, but he decided that if he built them himself, he could save the company a great deal of money, as well as make a little extra for himself. He started building shelves from the timber he bought at the local timber yard, shelves that would hold the future merchandise.

His bed, for the first few weeks, was a pile of straw in a room at the back of the shop, but as his image improved in his mind, he built himself a cot and bought a horsehair mattress which he felt was the height of luxury. His bathroom was a tap of ice cold water in the backyard. He was happy, and for the first time in a year he calculated that very soon he would be able to send for Chana. He knew it was impossible to send for her now. Only two years of the three had passed and although he lived frugally and counted all his pennies, he still did not have enough money to pay for her ticket. He worked hard, putting in long hours, and as the months passed the store grew in stature and size. His wages gradually rose as the store's turnover improved.

"I made lots of money," he told David the next day, after they had walked for some time, "but I became very lonely. Let me tell you, to be lonely is a terrible thing," and then almost as an afterthought he added softly, "and it makes you forget."

David's curiosity was aroused. This was the second time Meish had referred to loneliness and how it had affected him. He watched Meish carefully as they walked, waiting for him to explain what he meant, but Meish did not say anything to elaborate. He walked slowly, deep in thought, his eyes to the ground. Every now and then he would stop and dig in the sand with his cane as though he had found something of interest. This was not the Meish that David had come to know on their walks—something was troubling him. David, always the willing listener, instinctively knew that when Meish was ready, he would tell him what was on his mind. He also knew that whatever Meish would tell him was something he had never told anyone before.

Meish often repeated himself, not remembering where he was in his story, and David had to try and guess at a time sequence. The next day while they walked, he was once again reminiscing about how he had come to Koster. Having heard it all before, David was only half-listening when Meish said very slyly, looking at him out of the corner of his eye. "I haf never yentzed [had intercourse] so much in my life, as I did in that year in Koster."

David stopped in his tracks, not quite believing what he had heard. Meish shuffled on slowly, chuckling to himself.

David caught up with him. Meish was still chuckling, with a gleam in his eye.

"Ja those were interesting times. I forgot who I was and where I came from."

David walked silently at his side, wide-eyed with amazement at the confidence given. After a while Meish continued with his story.

Living in the back of the shop as he did, Meish found that he was unacceptable to the Koster Jewish community. They rarely invited him to their homes for a meal, and did not socialize with him. Koster had only four Jewish families, and even though he was good-looking, unmarried and Jewish, he was not considered good enough for their daughters, so they were inclined to ignore him. He had to establish himself first. By now he was twenty-three years old and definitely not looking for a wife. He was quite happy to be left alone. His memories of Chana were always in his mind. "I vanted to mek my fortune," he was fond of saying, "as qvickly as I cood."

His role model was Dasser, whom he still visited whenever he had the chance, as Brakenstroom was not that far from Koster. In his eyes, Dasser was a man who led a very respectable life, was wealthy, and was everything that he himself wanted to be.

He found it difficult to make friends in Koster, probably because of his accent and his appearance, as he spent very little money on his clothes. He had learned enough Afrikaans to serve his customers and give them the correct change, but he was lonely, and would often try and keep them in the shop, simply to talk.

Eventually he befriended a young Afrikaner, called Gerhardus. Gerrie worked for the timber yard where he had bought the timber for the shop. He introduced Meish to the local fishing hole and taught him to catch Geel Vis, the name given to a yellow carp found in the rivers, and Barbel, a type of catfish. Both were very bony, but Barbel was only eaten if you were truly hungry, most fishermen threw them back into the river. They would skewer them and braai (barbecue) them on an open fire on the river bank, under one of the many willow trees, enjoying the hot summer days and each others' company. Gerrie also taught Meish how to drink mampoer, 99% proof peach brandy, a potent homemade brew distilled from the yellow peaches that grew wild in everyone's backyard, a drink that Meish enjoyed even to this day, although he liked it better if he flavoured it with a touch of cherry brandy.

Meish, in turn, taught Gerrie the art of spicing his foods with garlic and the technique of pickling the local cucumber that grew prolifically in the hot South African sun whenever a seed was planted. For the first time since he came to South Africa, life was wonderful, and Chana took up less and less of his thoughts. Meish started to like Koster, partly because he was now earning a living but more particularly because he had a friend.

And then he caught the eye of Annatjie Schoeman, the station-master's wife. She had been one of his first customers, coming into the store more often than was necessary. Annatjie was about twenty-five years old, married to a man who had worked his way up from fireman on a steam engine to the position of station-master. Hendrik was an Afrikaner descended from the Voortrekkers, the name given to the pioneers who had fled by ox-wagon from the Cape to escape British rule, settling in the Transvaal and the Orange Free State. To be a descendant of the Voortrekkers was the height of snobbery. He took his position in life very seriously, and with his promotion to station-master, he soon become an ouderling (elder) in the Church, and started spending a great deal of time at various meetings with all its attentive duties.

Annatjie was fifteen years younger than her husband and less inclined towards his civic activities than he would have liked her to be. As time passed, the excitement of being married to the town's stationmaster waned and Koster with its small town social life bored her. She had had many flirtations with both married and unmarried men in the town, and had even had an affair with one of them, but after a while even that had bored her. She wanted more, a lover that worshipped her, not the male chauvinism of the Afrikaner men who believed that God made women to serve them. Meish, a young, good-looking foreigner whose store excited her with all its promises of the Johannesburg social scene, gave her the romantic dreams she craved. He became an obsession, so much so, that it was she who seduced Meish. The fact that he was a Jew troubled her at first, because the Dominee (Minister) had taught them that it was the Jews who crucified Christ, but . . . he was so good-looking.

"He must be different from all the other Jews," she would console herself.

She had noticed that Meish and Gerrie were friendly, and on the pretext of needing shelves for her kitchen, she walked into the timber yard. While Gerrie served her, she carefully steered the conversation towards Meish.

"I see that you are friendly with that Jew in the shop," she commented. "What type of a man is he?"

Gerrie, quick to realise that her question was based on more than idle curiosity, replied cautiously.

"Just like any other man, even better than some of those I know around here," he mumbled.

"He must be different to the other Jews then," she said casually, looking at him out of the corner of her eye to see his reaction, as she pretended to inspect some shelving. "The other Jews that live here stay with themselves, but you and . . . uh . . . Mr. Liebwitz," she mispronounced Meish's name, tinting it with an Afrikaans accent "are quite friendly."

"Ja," Gerrie answered, not quite sure of where she was leading him. He had heard stories about her flirtations every now and then, but he had usually dismissed them as sour grapes. She was a beautiful woman, and many of his drinking friends, on hearing stories about her, had expressed their envy, but nothing was ever confirmed. Her affairs were for the most part rumour, and then usually without much fire.

"Meish is a good ou (person). He is honest, and makes me laugh. I like him."

She nodded at his answer, asked him whether he would give her a quote on installing shelves in her kitchen, and then left as quickly as she could. She had learned what she had wanted to learn. Gerrie liked Meish—he had not spoken ill of him even though he was a Jew.

Gerrie teased Meish about Annatjie's interest in him and Meish, still very much the innocent, brushed off his jibes as pure imagination. Nevertheless, when Annatjie walked into the shop a few days later, Meish was very self-conscious and tried to serve her as quickly as possible. She, on the other hand, would not be brushed off and as soon as she saw another customer walk into the shop she said to him in broken English, "Please, go and help that customer there. I will look around a bit."

She gradually made her way towards the back of the shop, and as soon as she saw that his back was turned, she went into his living area. Meish had by this time bought several odd pieces of furniture, but his rooms were drab and most unattractive. She was shocked at what she saw.

When she slipped back into the shop, she had already formulated a plan to get to know him better. She waited until he came back to serve her.

"Mr. *Libwitch*," she said, trying to impress him with her English, "I think that I am one of your best customers." She waited for a sign of agreement from Meish, but did not receive one. "I also pay cash, and I do think that by now, I should get a cash discount on what I buy."

Meish said nothing. No customer had ever asked him for a discount before. He was not sure how to handle her request.

"You give me a . . . a . . . discount," she struggled to translate the word from Afrikaans to English, "and I will give your shop that little . . ." she found the translation to English too much for her, and switched into speaking Afrikaans, "what do you say, uh . . . artistic touch that it needs."

"What do you mean?" Meish asked in Afrikaans, not understanding her. In the short while he had been in Koster, he had picked up enough Afrikaans to make himself understood.

"Well, your windows for one," she replied. "Your display could be a lot better, also the inside of your shop, a display here and there would help sell more goods."

Meish was astute enough to realise that what she said made good sense. "Let me show you what I can do,"she continued, "and if you like it, then you can give me a job. Not full time," she added quickly as she saw him hesitate, "about two days a week. If you like what I do, then we can talk further."

Meish hesitantly agreed and Annatjie started work the next day. She was good at display and in the next two to three weeks the shop began to take on a more professional look. Sales improved and Meish felt that he had made a good decision. Annatjie was attractive and had a good sense of humour, and he found himself looking forward to the days she came to work. It wasn't long before she moved from decorating his shop to furnishing his living quarters. She made him order material for curtains, and at her insistence he even bought new clothes and started dressing with a great deal more care.

It did not take her long to seduce him. She had planned a visit to Johannesburg over the same weekend as one of his monthly business visits. She had sat with him in the same compartment on the train and made sure that he had helped her with her luggage once they arrived in Johannesburg.

That much David coaxed out of Meish. He couldn't get any more information no matter how hard he tried. Whether she seduced him on the train or whether it was at a hotel in Johannesburg, he could not find out. What he did realise, though, was that she was the first woman he had sex with, even though he had worked in a brothel while in London.

This was the start of their affair. Annatjie was a beautiful and sophisticated woman and Meish, a very presentable young man. She was lonely and bored, looking for the excitement an illicit affair would give her—she wanted to live the romantic stories she was so fond of reading. Meish was not lonely, he had his friend Gerrie and his business that took up more time than he had, but he had no female company and was totally inexperienced with women. To Annatjie, Meish was an uncut diamond that she enjoyed cutting and polishing to her own pattern. It was the story of Professor Higgens and Eliza Doolittle, but in reverse.

She redid his rooms, giving them that much-needed feminine touch, making sure that there were thick curtains on the windows of the bedroom, so that their frolicking escapades were private and performed in the luxury of pleasant surroundings. She also started taking Hendrik to work every morning and then stopping at the shop on the way back to her house, before Meish opened the doors for the day's trading. Her sexual appetite seemed almost boundless—she could not have enough of him.

Then again, on those evenings when Hendrik performed his church duties, she would sneak out of her house by the back door, making sure that no one would see her, leaving the children with Johanna, the maid. Meish never dared to go to her home. To visit a married woman without her husband being present was dangerous, especially in a town as small as Koster, so she went to him and, to use his favourite expression, they "yentzed, and yentzed and yentzed."

With love and patience she slowly turned this rather rough young man who only knew how to dress in the dark dreary attire of the religious Jew of the shtetl, into a man that took pride in dressing well and fashionably—a man that looked after his appearance. He had not become less religious, on the contrary, perhaps as a form of atonement for yentzing with a shiksah (non--Jewish girl) and somebody else's wife at that, he attended prayer services even more frequently than before.

As his clothing sense and manners improved at Annatjie's insistence, so he became more and more acceptable to the local Jewish community, who now started gossiping about which daughter he was going to marry. The only person who knew about his affair with Annatjie was of course Gerrie, who secretly enjoyed the way Meish was thumbing his nose at that town prig, the stationmaster.

"If that self-righteous ass only knew," he would laugh when he and Meish sat sipping mampoer.

Meish would swear him to silence and Gerrie, possibly a little jealous of Meish's success with Annatjie, would tease him even more by telling him that he would publish it anonymously in the local rag.

"Man, but the people in this town would get a lovely surprise if they only knew," he would say in Afrikaans, shaking his head. "They would have enough gossip to keep them going for years," and he would laugh long and loudly, enjoying his participation in the affair.

Meish began to lead a very demanding life. He was making love to Annatjie in the early mornings and again in the evenings whenever she was able to slip out of her house. He worked hard at the shop during the day and accepted social invitations only on those evenings when Annatjie had to play the part of a dutiful wife. She still worked for him in the shop, although not as often as she used to, but when she did, they were very careful not to show their affection towards each other. She was Mrs. Verster, and he was Mr. Liebowitz, but when they were alone with each other, she couldn't seem to have enough of him. He started to feel tired and his continual exhaustion started to affect his work.

"You see that katvis [small octopus] lying there," Meish pointed to a dead octopus that had washed up on the beach. "She was like that. I was caught by all her tentacles and I couldn't get away." As an afterthought he added, "But then, perhaps, I don't think I wanted to get away. The only thing is, what started off as fun was no longer fun. I didn't know what to do. It was nice to have her with me, but I also wanted to spend more time with Gerrie. You know, a man can't be with women all the time. He must also be with his male friends."

He tried to kick the dead creature as his memories flooded back and he nearly fell. David hurried forward to catch him, but Meish shook him off angrily. "It was enough!" he shouted as though warning David to back off. "It had to stop."

Something eventually did give. Annatjie fell in love with Meish and became extremely jealous of his visits to the Jewish community.

"You are going to marry one of those Jewish girls," she would say to him while she lay in his embrace, "and then you are going to forget all about me. You won't want me anymore." She would throw herself at him and make violent love to him.

"Annatjie," he would whisper, "why are you so angry? You are married, one day I will also marry."

She lay in his arms, her head on his chest, not saying anything. "Yes, one day I will marry," he continued softly, "I will marry, and start a family." She buried her head in his shoulder and cried. He kissed her forehead and she snuggled closer.

Annatjie became so obsessed with Meish that she found being married to her conservative Afrikaner husband stifling. She knew that she was behaving unreasonably, but she wanted more than simply an affair. She wanted some type of a commitment. She began to lose weight, stopped looking after her appearance, and became generally listless. Worst of all, she started to become careless in her visits to him. In a town as small as Koster, it was not long before the rumours began, which was more than she could bear.

Husbands are usually the last to find out about unfaithful wives, and Hendrik was no exception. She noticed that he became very quiet whenever they sat down together for a meal. He always seemed to have something on his mind, and he was beginning to treat her with less than his usual respect.

"I am sure he knows," she said to herself. Then, one night at dinner, as she sat deep in thought, toying with her food, he said gruffly, keeping his eyes on his plate, "I think we should have another child."

She looked up, not quite sure that she had heard him correctly.

"What . . . what did you say?" she asked, confused.

"I said that I think that we should have another child," he repeated, and he placed his hand over hers and looked into her eyes.

She couldn't meet his gaze, her eyes dropped. She looked down at his hand where it held hers. It was rough and callused, the skin burned horny by the sun when he had worked as a labourer on the track. She compared it in her mind with Meish's hand, hands that were soft and smooth from all the creaming she gave them, his nails beautifully manicured by her. She looked up into her husband's eyes and saw the incredible love he felt for her, and she knew that he knew about her affair. She turned her hand, so that her palm was in his, and then closed her fingers so that she held his hand tightly.

"Yes, Hendrik," she replied, straightening up in her chair. "You are right, we must have another child," and lifting his hand to her lips, she kissed his palm and with tenderness closed each of his fingers around her kiss.

"She told me all about it," Meish said to David, his voice trembling with emotion. "She told me that when she looked at his hand lying in hers she saw strength, the strength of a man that she needed, a man who loved her. She said that I was too soft for her, that I didn't love her. She had to be loved, to be dominated, and I was too young for that."

Meish spoke very softly and David had to strain to hear him.

"I suppose in a funny way I did love her," he continued, finding a seat on the steps of one of the many changing room cubicles that lined the Muisenburg beach. "But I never loved her the way I loved Chana. It was strange," he shook his head at the thought, "that a man can be in love with two women, but in different ways. I loved Chana, simply to be with her, to hold her, to smell her, to listen to her, that was enough, but with Annatjie it was a love that had to be consummated, that always ended with sex. She never ever said to me 'Meish, that is it, no more. We must stop.' She just waited." He shook his head slowly. "She must have wanted one more night with me," he continued, his eyes focussed on the horizon. "It was as though she needed a memory. It was only much later that I realised that this was our last night together."

She had her back to him, so that he couldn't see the expression on her face when she said, "Either I must divorce Hendrik, then we will get married . . . or I must go away for awhile."

He sat on the bed looking at her as she combed her hair, not knowing what to say.

Later, when he thought about the evening, he realised that had she approached him over a candlelit dinner, or gradually coaxed a proposal out of him, he might have married her; but at that moment he had been totally unprepared . He sat dumbfounded while she waited for him to say something. What she mistook for rejection was merely his attempt to clear his thoughts. However, by the time he was able to answer her, she had already finished dressing. She leaned over him, kissed him on the forehead, and murmured, "Totsiens liefie, ek gaan plaas toe. Ek moet my lewe herstel, want ek is swanger." [Goodbye my love, I must go to the farm. I must try and get my life back into order, because I am pregnant.]

Although by now he could speak and understand a little bit of Afrikaans as long as it was spoken slowly, he never quite understood what she had whispered because she had spoken fast, and very softly. She had kissed him on the cheek, and walked out of the room before he could ask her what she had said. He remembered the last word, swanger (pregnant) and asked Gerrie what it meant. From that day on, the thought that he could be the father of her baby worried him, but he never ever saw her again so that he could find out for certain. She had left Koster.

He asked Gerrie to find out where she was, but Gerrie refused.

"She probably wants to be away from you for the moment," Gerrie said, brushing him off. "Leave her. When she is ready she will know what to do."

After a great deal of thought, Meish decided that he must talk to his good friend Dasser, who, after listening to Meish's story, advised him to spend some time with him in Brakenstroom.

"A change of scenery will do you good," he advised. "Come stay with us for a while. We would love to have you."

Meish had worked two years without a holiday and had accumulated a backlog of paid leave. As soon as relief arrived from Johannesburg to look after the shop, he travelled to Brakenstroom where he stayed with Dasser. He spent his days and nights playing bridge, keeping his mind busy with thoughts other than that of Annatjie but, at the end of the month, when he should have returned to Koster, he found the memories of living there too painful. He travelled to Johannesburg, and resigned his position.

While Meish was telling David this, his angina pains returned. He placed a pill under his tongue as he usually did, but this time it did not seem to relieve his pain. David ran to a car parked near the beach for help. The driver was kind enough to give them a lift back to the apartment. Meish's pains started subsiding, but Getrude insisted that he lay down and rest.

"There is no need to call a doctor," Gertrude whispered to David once Meish was asleep. "These attacks have been pretty frequent lately, and after he lies down for a few minutes, they usually pass. The doctor warned me that he could go at any moment."

A few days passed before David had the opportunity to speak to Meish again, but he was once again the "crazy" Meish from Brakenstroom, not the Meish that he had come to know on the beach. It took another two days before he insisted that he wanted to walk on the beach again. David was scared to take him, but Gertrude said that he should.

When they reached the beach, Meish walked to the water's edge and stood looking out over the sea.

"I never ever saw her again," he said as he stared into the distance.

David knew that he was referring to Annatjie.

"I wrote to Gerrie about her often, but he told me that she never came back to Koster, and that Hendrik, her husband, was transferred. He could never find out where."

He looked very old and fragile, and David was scared to say anything in case he destroyed Meish's train of thought.

"You know, Dov," (he always called David by his Hebrew name) "wise men say that you must forget what happened in the past and always look forward into what is there, in the future." He pointed to the blue mountains that hovered in the early morning mist, on the opposite side of the bay. "But when you get old," he continued, "you live with your memories. I remember Koster like it was yesterday. I don't think I truly loved Annatjie, but I enjoyed making love to her. God punished me for that because I was made for and belonged to my Chana." He shook his head slowly from side to side. "One day soon, I will meet Him, and I will ask Him why? Why did He punish me? I don't think I did anything wrong. Was it a sin to make love to a woman I didn't truly love?"

A large wave washed up the beach, the water splashing around their ankles. David took Meish's arm, scared that he would lose his balance.

"Your grandfather," Meish continued, "was a very respected man. He was chairman of the shul committee. Because I stayed with him, people got to know me. That was how I met Aaron."

Aaron Miller had asked Meish to join him in establishing a malt factory in Brakenstroom. Meish had known nothing about malt, but he liked Aaron, who promised to teach him everything he knew, and he agreed. This was the start of his fortune, because in the years that he worked with Aaron, they built the factory into one of the largest suppliers of malt in southern Africa. Meish became a very wealthy man.

He looked again at the distant mountains. A tear welled in the corner of his eye and he brushed it away angrily, then turned and shuffled slowly back to the car.

In the days to come, they often had a whisky together in the evening and only occasionally walked the beach in the early morning. David tried to encourage Meish to finish the story, but he had lost him again, and couldn't get through to the Meish who had earlier poured his heart out to him. He felt cheated, because the story was incomplete—he wanted to know how it ended. There were so many questions left unanswered. He wanted to know how God had punished Meish and why Meish felt so strongly about it. He also wanted to know how Meish could have had an affair with Annatjie when he was so in love with Chana. What had happened to Chana? Did he ever see her again? He decided to talk to Gertrude.

One morning as they sat on the Muisenberg beach, he asked her.

"In my walks with your father on the beach," he started carefully, "he told me about a Chana he had left in Poland. Would you know about her?"

Gertrude became excited. "You mean he told you?" she said sitting bolt upright in her deck chair. "How wonderful. I always thought he had forgotten. It must be the sea air that has brought back his memories."

"Do you know what happened to her?" he asked.

"Oh yes," she replied, and then she reached over and put her hand on his knee. "She was my mother. Meish called her Chana, but here in South Africa they Anglicised her name. They called her Anne, or Annie. Did he tell you how he kidnapped her?"

"Kidnapped her?" David exclaimed loudly. "No, he told me nothing like that. He just told me that he left her in the shtetl in Poland."

"Well, he didn't exactly kidnap her," Getrude explained, "but it is so much more romantic to say that he did. She actually went with him willingly."

"Will you tell me the whole story from the beginning?" David asked hesitantly, expecting her to refuse.

"Of course" she replied, "I would love to. It is a wonderful love story. My mother often told it to me when she put me to bed at night when I was a little girl. I loved hearing it over and over again." She settled back into her deck chair and thought for a few minutes. "Now, where shall I begin."

David was pleased. The story would be complete.

4

"YOU DO KNOW THAT MEISH came to South Africa to make his fortune," she began, "and that everybody in the shtetl thought that he was in America."

"Yes," David answered, "Meish told me that on our walks."

"Well," she started, "Chana, my mother, waited for him to send for her." David leaned back in his deck chair contentedly, absorbing her every word.

"In all the time he was in South Africa she never once received a letter from him. In the first year, while he was struggling to make a living, he wrote to her every day, but he had no money to post the letters. He kept them all, and later, when they were married, he gave them to her as a wedding present. They are beautifully written love letters, and I treasure them. I will let you read them, if you want to, when we get back to Johannesburg."

"I would love to read them," David replied.

"When he went to Koster," she continued, "he worked so hard that he had no time for anything, only work, but when he moved to Brakenstroom and started the malt factory, he wrote a letter to my grandfather, my mother's father. He told us that he was too scared to write to my mother, in case she was married."

Chana had at first pined for Meish, waiting for him to write to her. As the years passed, not knowing whether he was still alive, she gradually tried to put him out of her heart and to forget about him. She couldn't. In the first year of their separation, she had cried herself to sleep almost every night as the romantic imagination of a young girl made her love for him larger than life. She had often visualized him arriving in the village in a fancy horse and carriage. She would climb in beside him and they would ride off to America. She knew it was a dream, one that would never become a reality, but she warmed herself with her daydream, wrapping it like a warm shawl around her thin shoulders.

When the letter Meish wrote from Brakenstroom did arrive, she was hurt that it was to her parents and not to her. In the three years since Meish had left her, she had grown taller and slimmer and more beautiful than ever before. Her memories of him and her love for him had given her that air of sadness and mystery that tore at the heartstrings of many a young man who met her.

"Papa," she said to her father, after having looked at the envelope addressed to him, "this letter is from South Africa. Is that not where Chaim went to?" Chaim had been a young Rabbi in the shtetl who had travelled to Durban in South Africa to become the Rabbi at one of the large synagogues there.

"Yes," he answered, "looking at the envelope, and then he asked reflectively, "I wonder why Chaim has written to me."

He opened the envelope carefully, so as not to destroy the stamps, and read the letter while Chana watched him. He put it down on the table next to him, closed his eyes for a few minutes, and then read it a second time. It was only one page, but he needed the time to think. She was still watching him, waiting for him to say something. He looked at her.

"It is not from Chaim," he said slowly.

"If it is not from Chaim, then who is it from?' she asked, curious at his hesitation.

"Here," he said after a few moments, and handed it to her, "read it."

She took the letter from his hand and glanced at the name of the writer. The blood drained from her face. Her hand and legs trembled. She sat down quickly and then read the letter. It was from Meish.

At first she felt overjoyed at reading it, but then she experienced a pang of disappointment. Why had Meish not written to her? Why had he written to her father?

"Papa," she whispered, "this letter is from Meish. He is in South Africa."

He looked at her and knew her confusion. She still loved Meish. He could see it in her face. He had hoped that she had forgotten Meish. In the past three years she had hardly spoken about him and he was sure that the Almighty had answered his prayers. Now, with one letter, all that was gone. He saw that she loved Meish as much if not more than before.

She reread the line that asked, "How is Chana?" then she folded the letter carefully and placed it close to her heart. Her father, who had been watching her closely, said nothing. He could feel the torment she was experiencing. He wished he knew how he could comfort her.

She stood up, composed herself, and said, "I will make you some tea." She walked out of the room into the kitchen, an excuse to get away from his searching eyes.

That night she read the letter over and over again looking for some sign that Meish still loved her, but there was nothing other than his question as to her well-being. Her tears stained the letter and the writing blurred as she wept uncontrollably. Eventually she put the letter on the table next to her bed and buried her face in the pillow to muffle her sobbing.

Chana's father had continually begged her to accept the advances of one of many young men in the village, but she couldn't bring herself to even think of loving another man. She was never short of suitors, but she felt that there was no one that she could love the way she loved Meish. She had loved him all her life, even in her dreams—there could be no one else. She read and re-read his letter and wrote many in reply, but she never posted them and tore them up—she felt that had Meish wanted her, he would have written to her and not to her father.

"The person I marry will be someone I could never love," she said to herself, "because no one can ever take Meish's place in my heart."

"Rachel in the Bible was prepared to wait fourteen years for Jacob," she often thought. "Perhaps three years are too short for me to wait for Meish. Perhaps I should wait longer."

By the fourth year, when Meish had still not written to her, she began to accept that he had forgotten her. She reluctantly gave in to her father's demands that she should at least look at the proposals of some of her suitors, but she always had some excuse or other as to why she could not accept any of them as a husband.

To see Chana was to love Chana. Her beauty had become ever more striking as she grew older. She was thin, perhaps overly so, and her height made her look thinner than she actually was. She was taller than most of the women in the village, in fact even taller than most of the men. Word of her beauty had spread to the other villages, and there was a steady stream of prospective suitors at her father's door.

Gersham came from the next village. He was a quiet man, preferring his own company to that of others. He spent his days studying the Talmud, a very sacred book that was probably written during the middle ages when Jews were placed in ghettos and forbidden from attending University. They turned inward, and studied the words of God and the laws handed down by Moses and the Rabbis that followed him. Gersham wanted to be a Rabbi like his father. He was the second son of Rabbi Yitzchak Rabinowitz and, although he never developed his father's ability to sway audiences with his sermons, he had earned the respect of the community as a learned scholar.

Had he known that the Rabbi would approach Chana's father on his behalf, he would have forbidden it, because although he had seen Chana on occasion, quietly admiring her beauty, he had never ever considered himself a worthy suitor.

When his father eventually told him that he had spoken to Avrom Hershowitz, Chana's father, and that a meeting had been arranged for the coming week, he was flabbergasted, blushing at the thought of his parent's audacity. He ran to the synagogue to pray to the Almighty and to collect his confused but excited thoughts.

"What a wonderful thing it would be," he prayed, pulling absentmindedly at the stringy hairs of his fledgling beard. "What a wonderful thing it would be if she accepted me for her husband,"

and he stared at his prayer book, his emotions a mixture of excitement and fear.

Eventually the day came for the meeting. In his nervousness he once again expressed his inadequacy of winning a beauty such as Chana, but the great Rabbi, unaccustomed to anyone in the village disagreeing with him, especially his son, brought his fist down hard on the kitchen table.

"You will come with me," he roared "and there will be no argument. The good Lord, Blessed be His Name, has shown me that she will be a good daughter to me and that you will be her husband. She comes from a fine family and will bear you many children. My grandchildren."

Gersham knew the look on his father's face, especially when his fist almost split the solid wood table. Such a gesture was finality in any discussion. Obediently, he went to his room and dressed in his best suit of clothes, the suit he wore only on the Sabbath.

He walked the ten odd miles to the next village behind his father, who led the way riding a donkey. The closer they came to the Hershowitz household, the more nervous he became. When they eventually arrived, Avrom Hershowitz flung open the door and welcomed the Rabbi into his household. Gersham, cringing behind the father, was not to be seen.

Chana was horrified. Her parents had told her of the meeting only one hour before. They had been scared that she would disappear as she had all the other times. They knew that she did not want to marry a Rabbi, even though her father was one. It would mean she would have to shave her head and wearing a sheitel (the wig worn by Orthodox women after they were married). It also meant being continually pregnant, because the Bible commanded, "Be fruitful and multiply."

"It is a great honour for Rabbi Yitzchak Rabinowitz to want you as the wife of his son," her mother had said.

"But Mama," she cried, "why must I marry? Why can't I always stay at home and be with you?"

"No, no, my child," she replied. 'As much as I love you, you must have a family of your own."

The two women stayed in the kitchen, leaving the men to themselves, but when Chana heard the Rabbi's booming voice, her curiosity got the better of her. She pulled aside a corner of the drapes that served as a door and looked for Gersham. Her father sat with his back towards her. On his left the Rabbi sat in his favourite chair, while Gersham sat on his right, his back to the window. He looked very uncomfortable, and fidgeted while the two men spoke.

She studied this man who wanted to be her husband. What she saw was not displeasing. He looked shorter than she, being slightly stooped from bending over his books. His skin was pasty white almost translucent, a sign that he spent a great deal of his time in the dim light of the shul, studying the Talmud. His shock of brown hair had a skull cap perched precariously on its crown, and his mouth trembled as he sat listening to his father. She felt both sorry for him and at the same time slightly amused at his discomfort.

She looked at the great Rabbi, whose booming voice extolled the virtues of being associated with his family.

"If only he had a bit of the fire his father has," she whispered to her mother, as they huddled together spying on the men through the kitchen doorway. Eventually, rejecting him as a suitor, she turned away to prepare the sweet tea her father had told her the Rabbi liked.

Then she heard the Rabbi say, ". . . and they will live in South Africa. I have a cousin there, living in a town called 'Yohaanisburg.' He wrote that the Shul was in need of a Rabbi."

Without thinking, she put down what she was doing and calmly walked into the sitting room, sat down next to her father, looked Gersham straight in the eye and smiled. Her father, surprised at her joining them without being asked to, frowned at her behaviour and took her hand. Gersham turned bright red at her smile and jumped to his feet, knocking over his chair.

"This is my daughter Chana," Avrom said, slightly disoriented by her unexpected presence. He squeezed her hand, questioning her presence, and she squeezed his in return and looked at him and smiled, conveying her acceptance. This surprised him, because he did not think that she would accept Gersham as a suitor.

"My dear, don't you think you should make the Rabbi and his son some tea?"

"Yes Papa," she said humbly and, giving Gersham another smile that left him almost idiotic in his adoration of her, left the room.

Six months later, after Gersham had been ordained as a Rabbi amidst as much pomp and ceremony as the little village had ever seen, they were married. Within the week, they left for South Africa.

5

MEISH STOOD BEFORE THE open window of his room, looking out into the garden. It was summer. There had been less rain than average this year, but with the new dam that had been built on the Brak River, the town had plenty of water, water that was led to the gardens by a web of furrows that lined the streets. The branches of the fruit trees were breaking with the weight of the heavy fruit, and the flowers, in spite of all the water, wilted in the hot sun. In Meish's hand was a letter he had received from Chana's father. He had written all about Chana's wedding, telling Meish how lucky she was to have married a Rabbi's son. He also wrote that they were going to live in Johannesburg.

"He will be the Rabbi in the new shul," he had written. "Perhaps you know of it. It will be good to hear from you . . . and please," he had added in what almost appeared to be an afterthought, "look after her, for the sake of the friendship between our two families. Remember that your father and I were children together."

Meish could not read any more. The dreams of his youth and of Chana came flooding back. He had forgotten her and worst of all, he had forgotten his promise to her.

He remembered her beauty, her kindness and gentleness, how the children in the village always crowded around her wherever she walked. How everyone loved her. He remembered her smile and her laughter whenever he said something that amused her. He remembered the tilt of her head when she looked at him and the touch of her lips on his when she kissed him, and he felt sick at the thought of how he had betrayed her.

He had made a great deal of money as a partner in the malt factory, and dressed in the more fashionable styles of the year. He stood tall and hard work had made him lean and fit. The outdoor life had tanned his skin, putting a touch of auburn in his pitch-black hair. He was still unmarried, having been too involved in his work. His experience with Annatjie was something of the past, but her lessons in how to conduct himself in the company of women gave him a charm that was lacking in most other men. He had often felt that it was time to marry and yet, although his eye, casually cast over the daughter of many a prospective father-in-law, caused many a heart to flutter, he had not yet seen or found someone he wished to share the rest of his life with.

The letter from Chana's father aroused his curiosity. He became excited at the prospect of seeing Chana again, even though she was someone else's wife.

"I will be one of the crowd that welcomes them to Johannesburg," he told Dasser. "I must see what she looks like."

It did not take long to find out when they were expected. A letter to the chairman of the Johannesburg Hebrew Congregation confirmed the date and the train they would be arriving on. The train to Johannesburg from Cape Town passed through Brakenstroom. Meish decided that rather than travel to Johannesburg and welcome them at the station with the local congregants, he would join the train at Brakenstroom and travel with Chana and Gersham to Johannesburg. That way he would spend time with them alone before they became involved in the celebrations he knew would be waiting for them. Deep down he admitted to himself that the real reason for joining the train at Brakenstroom was that he was curious about Chana. He wanted to see how she had grown, how she wore womanhood. Was she changed or was she still the girl that he had loved in his boyhood? Had the years aged her in the way the hard life of the shtetl aged the women who lived there?

On the day she was due to arrive on the train, he dressed in his finest suit, a grey wool that Dasser had just recently tailored for him. As the engine puffed into the station, he rose from the bench where he was sitting, his carpetbag with a change of clothing in his hand. His heart started racing at the thought of seeing her, and he scoured each carriage window that passed, searching for a sign of her. He looked striking as he stood and waited. His light grey suit with white shirt contrasted with his deeply tanned face. A perfectly made ruby cravat around his throat gathered with a pearl tiepin was offset by a gold watch chain that caught the glint of the sun as it stretched across his waistcoat. He looked the epitome of the successful businessman that he had indeed become.

Chana had been sitting at the window of the carriage, looking at the endless veldt that had passed by, bored with the thought of the train stopping at yet another dusty town. The lack of rain had burned the grass yellow, and the khaki seemed to stretch forever into the distance, broken here and there by the odd bluegum or umbrella-like thorn tree. The continual soot from the engine was a constant irritant around her neck, where the high-collared long-sleeved dress she wore made her perspire freely in the hot South African summer. Her sheitel, which Gersham insisted she wear at every station, felt dirty, with the soot forming a black rim at her hairline.

The train window was open, in spite of Gersham's protestations that this would only bring in more soot, but the cool breeze caused by the train's forward motion was a small relief. She looked at the presentable man in the grey suit and, like the faithful wife that she was, especially the wife of a Rabbi, she cast her eyes downward. Then, just as quickly, she looked up again. She raised her hand to her lips as she recognised Meish, her heart leaping into her throat. She turned her eyes away, but her curiosity got the better of her and she looked at him again. This time his eyes caught hers. Her hand covered her mouth to stifle a scream and she almost fainted as the blood left her face.

Meish had been looking at every coach window as the train slowly came to halt. He saw this woman look at him, saw her raise her hand to her mouth and whiten perceptibly. She looked away, her hand shaking at her mouth.

"This is," he said to himself, "this can only be Chana."

His heart pounded in his chest with all the longing of five years. Beneath the clumsy black wig and the formal dress, he recognised the girl he remembered. He walked to the compartment window.

She turned to him, and for a brief moment her eyes met his again. He knew then that he loved her even more now than he had ever loved her before. She leaned back in her seat as though hiding from him. Where she had been pale a few seconds ago, she was now flushed and agitated.

"What is it, Chana?" Gersham asked. He was too involved with his reading to look out of the train window and it was only her agitation that had disturbed him.

"Nothing, Gersham," she answered with a slight quiver to her voice, as her emotions threatened to better her. "Just a little faint from the heat."

He turned back to the book he was studying, completely oblivious to her confusion. There was a knock at the door of the compartment.

She looked up as it opened. Meish stood in the doorway, his bag in one hand, a small bouquet of flowers in the other.

"Yes, can I help you?" Gersham asked in Yiddish, looking up from the book he was reading. Chana had turned her head away on seeing Meish and was trying to hide her emotions by looking out of the window. She could feel her pulse throbbing in her throat.

Meish looked at Gersham, who was watching him quizzically, waiting for an answer. He then looked at Chana, who kept her head turned from him. His reply, when it came, was soft with a note of uncertainty. He replied in Yiddish, his voice filled with emotion, but he addressed Chana, not Gersham as he should have done.

"Chana, it is I, Meish. I have brought you some flowers to welcome you to Brakenstroom."

Gersham looked more closely at Meish. He did not understand. He also did not see the fresh colour that had risen to his wife's face. The fact that this man called his wife by her name surprised him. He placed his book carefully on the seat beside him and stood up.

"You are from the congregation, yes?" he asked, not quite sure what to make of Meish. He bent to look out of the window, for more of the congregation. He had not expected this station would be Johannesburg. The porter had assured him that he would tell them when they reached their destination.

Because of this, he did not see Chana's confusion, nor the way Meish struggled with his feelings. When he eventually did turn to Meish after he had realised that Meish was the only person who had come to meet them, Meish had recovered his composure.

"Nu, are you the only one here to welcome us?" Gersham asked, standing as tall as he could, and trying to sound like his father.

Meish smiled, and for the first time since he had seen Chana, he relaxed.

"Good morning, Rabbi Rabinowitz," he said, extending his hand. "My name is Meish Leibowitz, and I am not part of the delegation to meet you, but I am from the congregation of Brakenstroom and would like to extend to you and your . . . er . . . wife," and he hesitated, "a welcome to our beautiful town. I am also going to Johannesburg, and thought I could accompany you, if that does not inconvenience you?"

Chana had noticed his hesitation. She had not turned her head when Meish welcomed Gersham and had remained looking out of the window at the people on the station. She smiled to herself and that smile broke her tension. She was sure Meish had found it difficult to refer to her as Gersham's wife and that pleased her. She moved her head slightly, so that she could look at him out of the corner of her eye.

"Ah, Meish . . ." Gersham said, taking Meish's out-stretched hand. Turning to Chana he continued excitedly, "Chana, this is Meishka . . . from your home town. What a wonderful surprise."

Within minutes and with little prompting from Meish, Gersham asked him to sit down. Storing his carpetbag on the upper luggage rack, Meish sat next to Gersham and immediately asked for news from home. He studiously ignored Chana, which was the custom, since a Rabbi's wife should not talk to another man. But she sat listening intently to his questions, her hands in her lap, her eyes scanning everything in the compartment, but avoiding him. She waited respectfully for her husband to answer all his questions.

Eventually Meish steered the conversation to answers only she could give. She had become, by this time, fully composed, and she told him all the latest gossip of the village. She reached into her bag and brought out a number of letters.

"These are for you," she said, handing them to him. As he reached for them his fingers brushed hers. It was as if an electric shock had passed between them. She looked at him, and found that he was looking intently at her. She withdrew her hand quickly, turning her head to look at the passing veldt, anything to escape his gaze. The letters fell to the floor of the carriage. Her chest heaved as she leaned forward to pick them up. Meish had also bent down as he tried to catch them, and their two heads almost collided. When he saw her ear close to his lips, without thinking he whispered, "I love you."

Chana stood up, her face white.

"Excuse me," she mumbled, "I . . . I . . . "

The rocking of the train as it started moving pushed her down hard in her seat, knocking her head against the backrest. The blow brought tears to her eyes. Within seconds Meish was next to her, all propriety forgotten as he dabbed at her sudden tears with a clean handkerchief, concern etched all over his face. She closed her eyes and leaned back, enjoying his presence next to her. She trembled and knew that she loved him even more now than she had ever loved him before.

Meish, suddenly realizing that he was comforting another man's wife, and a Rabbi's wife at that, quickly rose to his feet.

"I shall get her a glass of water," he said, and he stumbled from the compartment, leaving Gersham looking confusedly at his back.

He stopped in the aisle as though in a daze, turning slowly to the window. The countryside flew past him, but he did not see it as he gripped the brass rail that stretched the length of the carriage with both hands, his mind in total confusion.

Chana sat quietly, deep in her thoughts. She looked at Gersham thinking how he was and yet was not her husband—for although their marriage had been consummated, it had been an effort for her and a duty for him. He was more interested in the Talmud than in the world around him. Her reaction to Meish had surprised her. She had not realised how much she still loved him.

Chana waited for Meish to come back to the compartment, at the same time afraid at what would happen when he did. When he did not return after fifteen minutes, she became restless, worried that he would not return. After a half-hour she could wait no more. Telling Gersham that she was going to the washroom, she left the compartment to find him.

She saw him standing at the end of the carriage, leaning on the rail, looking into space. Timidly she approached him. He did not turn to look at her, but he felt her in every nerve in his body and shivered as she approached. She stood next to him, not saying a word, her shoulder brushing his as the train rocked its way through the veldt.

After a few minutes he said, without looking at her, "You do know of course, that you belong to me."

She replied softly, her heart throbbing in her chest. "Yes," she said, and then more hesitantly so that he hardly heard her, "but you forgot about that."

"I forgot about myself," he said, "but now that I have found you again, I can never let you go. You do know that also?"

She hesitated. "Yes," she whispered so softly that he almost did not hear her.

They stood next to each other, the clickity-clack of the train echoing their racing heartbeats. He placed his hand over hers where she gripped the rail tightly.

"Will you ever forgive me ?" he asked, turning towards her, his voice betraying the pain he was experiencing.

"No," she replied, her eyes blurred with her tears.

"Will you divorce Gersham and marry me?" he pleaded.

She stood looking at the moving countryside as though she had not heard him. He watched her anxiously, looking for some expression that would answer his question. He saw her brow furrow and then, as though tearing herself with great effort from the panorama that flowed past the train, she turned and gradually brought her eyes up to his. Her tears flowed freely down both cheeks, leaving furrows of soot. His heart beat with the anguish of despair. Then she smiled. He sighed and opened his arms. She moved into his embrace.

"Yes," she whispered, and, standing on tip toe, she kissed him on the side of his mouth.

They had walked back to the compartment and Meish helped her take down her suitcase from the luggage rack. She told Gersham that she was going to change her clothing. He was so engrossed in his reading that she doubted he had even heard her.

Soon after, the train stopped at a siding. Chana and Meish disembarked and waited on the platform as the train pulled out. They sat on their baggage hand in hand while she excitedly told him everything that had happened while he was away. He reached up tenderly, and took off her sheitel. Her long hair had been cut short. He kissed her tenderly, and she whispered. "It will grow back."

Three hours later, they caught the train from Johannesburg back to Brakenstroom.

"The story was that Meish had kidnapped her," Getrude said. "But Mama told me that if anybody had kidnapped anyone, it was probably she who had kidnapped him. It took seven months for her to obtain a 'get' [Jewish divorce], from Gersham, who at first refused, but later realised that it was better to give Mama her freedom, than to keep her married to him. All that time she lived with Dasser and Janie Asher, your grandparents. When they did marry, the wedding was a quiet one, attended by a few friends. I will never forget the words your grandfather said at the wedding. Mama would tell me over and over again. 'This was a love affair made in heaven.' he said, 'Nothing could keep them apart, although sometimes, the Almighty does move in strange ways. With Chana and Meish it took Him a little longer than is usual.' "

When Getrude recounted Dasser's words to David, tears came to his eyes.

"How did your mother die?"

"Very quietly, in her sleep," she replied. "One morning when Meish woke, he found her dead in the bed next to him. The doctor said that she had died from a burst aneurism. That is when Meish went mad. He kept saying that God had punished him for something he did when he first came to South Africa."

"How old was your mother when she died?" David asked. Although the pain showed in Gertrude's eyes, he had to know.

"She was fifty-nine," Getrude answered, "still a young woman."

She leaned forward and took his hand. "You know, Dave, I don't know what Meish told you on your walks. I don't want to know. But for the first time since Mama died, he was like the way I used to know him. When she died, so did he. Thank you for bringing him back, even if it was only for a moment." Her eyes brimmed with tears. "You did him a lot of good. Thank you."

Tzippie

1

MAX, DASSER'S ELDEST SON, was not the most brilliant of doctors. It had taken him almost eleven years to obtain his medical degree, four years longer than he should have taken. He had studied at the London Hospital, Whitechapel, a teaching hospital situated in the East End of London, England. It was a busy hospital, serving the less fortunate of London society. This did not detract from the quality of physicians who graduated; on the contrary, the very volume of work allowed them to see almost every disease that appeared in the textbooks of that time.

In the years that it took Max to qualify, he had the best of all medical worlds. He had always felt that it was not the difficulty of the medicine that made him take so long to qualify, it was simply that there was so much work that he had very little time to study. In a way this was true, because he was a dedicated doctor, born with a "bedside manner." Patients became personal friends, and he in turn became their physician, counselor, psychiatrist, and financial advisor. In other words, he became their General Practitioner. The result was that although Max was not a brilliant medical theorist, his practical knowledge combined with his patient empathy soon made him a very popular and much sought after physician.

When he eventually received his degree in medicine, he returned to Brakenstroom to start his practice. The people of the town soon learned to love him, and took full advantage of his rapport with his patients. Max was a good doctor, and his practice very quickly became so busy that he often forgot to charge his patients. He was a workaholic because he loved his profession. His patients, who were mostly farmers, became accustomed to paying him in kind rather than in cash, often deciding what they felt they owed him when they never received an account. His yard at home was a virtual chicken run full of feathered gifts, and one would often find a few hens in his consulting rooms, waiting to be taken home. His house was always full of fresh fruit and vegetables, but he gave most away to his staff and to those patients who were less fortunate. Homemade jam, canned peaches—all the delicacies of an Afrikaner kitchen could be found in Max's kitchen.

Although not strictly kosher, he kept the dietary laws where possible. Occasionally a patient who did not know that he was a Jew would bring him a half a sheep, a buck of biltong (raw dried meat, a South African delicacy) or even a pig. These he would pass on to his nurse, Marie, or any other patient who needed them. Her friends at the location regarded Jane, the black maid who looked after him, as having the most fortunate job in town. Although Max often forgot to pay her, she and her family always had plenty to eat.

Marie was not the brightest of nurses, and Max often wondered how she had managed to obtain her nursing diploma. She had virtually employed herself, simply moving in to his surgery to manage his appointments. Max was never quite sure who paid her salary because the practice brought in very little cash. She never ever asked him for money, although she was far from undernourished or poorly dressed. Max supposed she simply took what she needed, either in produce or in cash, if and when any money came in. On the other hand, she always saw to it that there was enough in Max's bank account, because whenever he wrote out a cheque, it was always met. He never ever doubted her honesty.

When Esme fell pregnant, it was only natural for her and Jerry to choose him as their doctor. Her labour pains started late in the afternoon with Jerry breaking almost every traffic law as he rushed her to the hospital. Max was waiting for them. He examined her immediately and told her that although she had not dilated fully, she was progressing well. Twenty hours later the baby's head finally moved into the birth canal.

"Take a deep breath and start pushing when I tell you to," Max told Esme. He could see the baby's head, but it did not look right. He frowned and looked down at the instrument in the midwife's hand as she read his thoughts, but he shook his head. He had never yet had occasion to use instruments in a delivery and he was not going to use them now. His small hands, which could easily slip into the birth canal, had served him better than any instrument in the past.

"Push . . . NOW!" he commanded Esme.

Esme pushed, but nothing appeared to happen. The baby simply did not want to be born. Esme's eyes rolled in her head as she looked up at the white hospital ceiling whenever she took a breath between contractions, and her face distorted as she tried to return the smile of the nurse that held her hand.

"Dear God," she moaned softly through clenched teeth, "let this be over. I don't know how much more I can take."

The perspiration ran down her face, and her lips moved in thanks to the nurse, who wiped her brow. She was exhausted and Max could see by her grimace that the pains of the contractions were becoming unbearable.

"Push one last time. Try as hard as you can," Max said to her, not showing the concern in his voice.

She pushed hard with the contraction and then screamed with pain. Then, suddenly, it was all over, and she lay back in total exhaustion. She took a shuddering breath and tried to ask if it was a boy. Jerry wanted a boy so much, but she felt far too tired to talk. The room darkened, and she closed her eyes.

The baby Max held in his hands was a girl, with a badly deformed head. It did not cry when he slapped it to stimulate breathing, so he slapped it again, a little harder. When she still refused to breathe, he started working on her. He had never lost a baby, and he had no intention of losing one now. Eventually she took a deep breath, and then lay limply on the examination table as she struggled to breathe. He handed her to the midwife, who washed the blood away tenderly. Max only then turned to Esme. Something had ruptured inside her with the delivery and she was hemorrhaging badly. She needed surgery urgently. Fortunately, Roy, who was a brilliant surgeon, was in the hospital and within minutes Esme was being wheeled into the operating theater.

Only then did Max examine the baby. He did not like what he saw and shook his head slowly. The baby's skull was elongated and badly squashed on one side. He performed all the usual reflex tests, but there was little if any response. That there was brain damage was without question.

Jerry knew something was wrong the minute he saw Max.

"How is Esme?" he asked, concern showing on his face as Max walked towards him from the delivery room.

"I have had to call in Roy," Max answered quietly. He did not have to explain to Jerry who Roy was. Brakenstroom was still small enough for everybody to know each other by first names.

"She is bleeding far too much, and I could not stop it."

Jerry felt the blood drain from his face.

"Will she be all right? Can I see her?" he looked anxiously at the door of the delivery room.

Max held him back. "She is already in theater and she will be fine. You know Roy, he is the best, and we are very lucky to have him here. Fortunately, he was at the hospital, and he came the minute I called him. I must join him now." He turned to walk away.

"And the baby?" Jerry asked almost as an afterthought. Max stopped at the door, turned slowly and looked at him.

"It is a little girl," he said, his eyes taking in the expression of joy that appeared on Jerry's face. "But," he continued, looking away, "she is not all right."

Jerry said nothing. He stood with his hands at his sides opening and closing his fists as he took in what Max had said. He looked down at the ground, crestfallen, then he looked up into Max's eyes.

"Is it dead?" he asked dully.

"No," Max answered, choosing each word with care. "*She* is not dead." He tried to give the baby an identity.

"Can I see it?" Jerry pleaded, ignoring Max's effort.

Max looked at him. He saw a man who had come to the hospital expecting to leave it with a wife and baby. Now he would be lucky enough to leave it with a wife.

"Why not?" he shrugged. "Come with me."

The nurse in the labour room was holding a small bundle in her arms. She placed it in a cradle as they walked in. Jerry glanced around the ward, looking for Esme. He saw a bloodstained sheet being folded by a nurse stripping the bed.

He shook his head and then walked hesitantly to the cradle to look at his daughter. He stretched out a finger towards a perfect tiny hand that lay motionless above the blanket, and marveled at its miniature perfection. He carefully opened the blanket and shuddered as he saw the baby's head and face. He turned away.

"What must we do?" he asked softly, as though to himself, his voice without emotion.

"Should the baby live, she should probably be placed in a mental home," Max answered, feeling Jerry's pain. "She did not respond to any of the tests I gave her. I believe that she is brain damaged, but I will ask a pediatrician to look at her and give an opinion."

Jerry turned his back to Max and walked across the room to the window. He looked out blankly into the early morning grayness as the first rays of the sun broke through the dark mantle of the night.

"It is remarkable," he grieved, his voice flat, devoid of all emotion. "The day starts just like any other day. To everybody out there, nothing out of the ordinary has happened."

He stood silently for a few minutes, then turned to face Max.

"I don't want Esme to see it," he said lifelessly. "Tell her . . . tell Esme that it died."

"Is that the right answer?" Max gestured towards the cradle. "Should the baby live and is placed in an institution, can you live with that decision on your conscience? Could your marriage survive? No, Jerry, think about it before your decision is final. I believe that Esme must know."

"Yes, I suppose you are right," Jerry whispered, turning away. "I will think about it."

"I must go to theater to see what is happening," Max said dejectedly, knowing that Jerry would not accept his advice. He walked from the room, his shoulders bowed with grief.

Half an hour later, he had to return to Jerry. He did not know how he could face him with tragic news for a second time. Everything had gone wrong in what should have been a very normal delivery. When he saw Max, Jerry rose.

"Esme?" he asked softly. The pain in his face was terrible to see.

"Esme is fine," Max answered, his face not reflecting his words.

"Thank God for that," Jerry replied, relieved, and for the first time that day he smiled. "Can I see her?"

"In a few minutes. Roy is just completing the operation." Max took Jerry by the arm. "Jerry . . ." he started. From the tone in Max's voice Jerry knew that something else was wrong.

"What happened in there?" he asked, concern once again etching his face.

"Roy could not stop the bleeding. He was forced to perform a hysterectomy to save Esme," Max said.

Jerry was silent as he digested what Max had told him. "This means that Esme can never have another baby?" he asked, his voice trembling with emotion. Max nodded. "But . . . is she all right?" he continued, squeezing Max's arm with his concern.

"Yes," Max replied, encouraged that Jerry had not broken down. "She will be fine."

Jerry breathed a sigh of relief. "Then that is all that counts," he shrugged, his action a mask of his true feelings. "It would be just too much to have lost her as well."

He took Max's hand and squeezed it hard. "Max, you're a damn good doctor. I appreciate everything you have done, even though the circumstances may not have been of the best. At least this nightmare is now over. Thank you." He started crying as the tension of the evening drained from him. "Now please, can I see Esme? I want to be with her when she wakes up."

The two men looked into each other's eyes. Max saw in Jerry a man with a difficult decision that still had to be made, a decision he had put aside for now, overjoyed that his wife was still alive.

2

AFTER WORKING FOR HIM FOR almost ten years, Marie met and married a colleague, Dr. Gunter Kasch, and very reluctantly left Max to run Gunter's practice and home.

"I am leaving you at the end of the month," she said to him as she brought him his tea between patients.

What she said didn't register. He was still thinking about the patient he had just seen.

"Gunter and I are getting married," she continued a little louder, pouring his tea, "and I will be helping Gunter in his practice. He is taking on the position of District Surgeon, and he needs me."

"What?" he asked, angry at being disturbed. "What did you say?"

"I said that Gunter and I are getting married, and that I will be leaving you," she repeated, not at all surprised that he had not heard her the first time.

"But you can't," he shouted, as the horror of her leaving dawned on him.

"I can't what?" she asked tersely. "I can't get married or I can't leave?"

"You can't leave," he replied desperately. He looked around his office, waved his hands and said, "What am I going to do when you leave? I can't manage all this without you."

"I have found someone to take my place. She will be here tomorrow so that you can meet her." Marie walked to the door with the tea tray, turned to look at him and continued, "And it's about time you also got married. Look at you. Your suit is dirty. Your tie is dirty and your shirt has not been properly ironed. You have also put on too much weight. You need a wife to look after you." She left the office and closed the door behind her, leaving him in a daze.

For a while, he was devastated. He had not realized how much he had relied on her. Her replacement was good, but simply was not Marie. Her leaving made him consider marriage for the first time. He was forty-five years old and slowing down, but above all, he was tired of coming home to an empty house. Jane, the maid, had been with the family for the last thirty years, and had kept house for him and his parents before him, but he was lonely. Marie was right. It was time he found a wife. Life just seemed to fly by.

He wasn't the best looking of men, with a heavy paunch and sparse graying hair. His voice was gruff and husky from all the cigarettes and cigars he had enjoyed smoking.

"I am sure I can make some woman happy," he thought. "If I can't make her happy, at least I can offer her security. There must be someone who will marry me."

He decided that he did not want someone with children. He wanted to have his own children, even at this late stage in his life. This made the task of finding a wife all the more difficult, for most of the single women that would have met his needs were either divorcees with children or were past childbearing age. Nevertheless he was adamant, and so he set about advertising for a wife in the only way he knew how. He told all his friends.

"And she must be a good cook . . ." he would add, after giving them his other specifications.

Once everyone in the town knew that "Doc" was looking for a wife, he had no end of helpers. They were not that confident of finding someone who would meet his standards, but the search gave them a discussion topic at many a social gathering. The wives of his friends moved in with a vengeance. They forced him to lose weight, insisted that his suits be clean, and started telling Jane how to run his home.

"If you don't get these other Ma'ams out of my house, I will leave." Jane shouted at him one day. "They all shouts at me and tells me something else." He stood thunderstruck, surprised that she could say anything other than "Yes master."

Soon there was a stream of women of all ages visiting his home, many to pass judgement on him and others, hoping he would favour them. This went on for almost six months. By this time, with all the nagging of his helpers, he often wished that he had kept his mouth shut. He had lost weight, wore a clean shirt every day, had Jane dust the cigar ash off his jacket lapels, and had become presentable to a degree. He even had his hair cut by a hairdresser, not the barber he had been using for the previous ten years. He found that he enjoyed the attention he was receiving and he liked his new image, but sometimes . . . .

"Oh for the peace and quiet of the good old days," he would muse, sucking a cigar.

Esther worked as a sister in the pediatric ward in one of Johannesburg's most prestigious hospitals. As a young girl, she had had her share of affairs, mostly with doctors, hoping that any one of these liaisons would lead to a more permanent relationship, but not one of them ever did. When she turned thirty-five and was still single, she became resigned to the fact that her chances of finding a husband were diminishing. She would have to marry one day, she decided, not for love, but for companionship.

"As long as he is kind and treats me well," she told all her friends. "He doesn't have to look like Clark Gable," and then with a twinkle in her eye, because she had a wonderful sense of humour, "but if he looked like Cary Grant, that would be an asset." This was probably the reason why she never married; she was simply too picky. Either that, or she had simply not met the man she wanted to spend the rest of her life with.

Then she met Carol Cohen. Carol lived in Brakenstroom, and had brought her son Ramon to Johannesburg for a tonsillectomy. It was not long before Carol and Esther were talking to each other as if they were long lost friends. Both were Jewish, so they had a common bond. Esther liked Carol, and when her shift for the day finished, instead of going home, she took Carol to the hospital canteen for a coffee.

When Carol asked her outright, "Are you married?" she felt that Carol was overstepping their new-found friendship.

"No, I am not." she replied tersely, and when she saw Carol's eyes light up as though pleased that she wasn't, she felt hurt, and so she told a white lie. "I have simply been too busy to spend the time looking for a husband."

"Well, then you would be perfect," Carol squealed, clapping her hands with delight. "Could I introduce you to a man who has the same problem you have? He is simply too busy to find a wife."

"As long as he is not a bore, does not spit when he talks, and is not old enough to be my father," Esther forced a laugh, trying to make light of it. "If he has a sense of humour, even all that may be bearable."

"Max a bore?" Carol looked astonished. "Good Heavens no. When we manage to get him to a party, he is the life and soul, and as for spitting, I have never seen him, but he does smoke cigars. I will have to arrange a date."

"It's a long time since I have been on a blind date," Esther said, shaking her head, "and quite honestly I don't think I would like to go on one at this time of my life."

But Carol would not accept a "no" for an answer.

That Friday afternoon, as she sat looking at the countryside from the window of the bus taking her to Brakenstroom, she had misgivings. She watched the green *mielie* (corn) and yellow sunflower fields fly past, but saw nothing as her thoughts were elsewhere. She felt sad—sad that her life had somehow passed by so quickly that she had to travel such a long distance simply to meet a man. She knew she was attractive, but then what was wrong with her that none of her boyfriends had ever proposed?

"Did I ever give them a chance to propose?" She wiped a tear from her eye, and opened the newspaper she carried with her and started solving the crossword puzzle as a way to stop feeling sorry for herself.

Max had accepted Carol's invitation to dinner. He liked Felix and Carol and knew that he would get a good meal, especially since the invitation was for Friday night. Carol did not mention that a second guest would be present, but she knew that Max always went to shul on a Friday night and took a little more care than usual in the way he dressed. She did not want Max to know that he would meet someone at her house. She wanted a casual meeting, without any pretensions on Max's part.

Felix had met Esther before shul, just after Carol had fetched her from the bus. He liked what he saw and he also liked the way Carol and Esther had developed such an easy friendship. Carol, he knew, was very choosy with her friends, and the fact that she had taken to Esther meant that Esther had to be someone exceptional.

His concern about Esther's impression of Max made him give Max a "once-over" at shul, and he casually dusted any cigar ash from Max's jacket.

"I suppose he looks good enough," he calmed Carol as he walked into their house. Max was still busy parking his car. "Thank God it is Friday night, and he is religious enough not to smoke on the Sabbath."

When Carol opened the door to Max, she also gave him a once-over, and muttered a prayer of thanks that his suit wasn't the old creased one he usually wore.

"Well, here goes," Carol whispered to Felix as they led Max to the lounge. "Let us hope it works."

Esther had washed and changed. She was sitting on the sofa talking to Ramon. She looked stunning. Her light brown hair sparkled with the light of the reading lamp that stood on the small table next to her. Her dress was a white chiffon, very summery and cut low to highlight the cleavage of a full bosom. Her skirt flared at the waist in a multitude of pleats, and her legs, possibly a little thin, were crossed at her ankles. Her hands, beautifully manicured with square cut nails that as a nurse she had to have, were casually turning the pages of a book that Ramon had given to her to look at.

Carol whispered to Felix as Max walked in ahead of them.

"If he doesn't fall for her then I simply don't know what."

Esther stood up as they walked in. She was a small woman, fine boned and a lot more petite than Carol had remembered, but then a nurse's uniform can hide a great deal.

"Max," Carol said walking to Esther and taking her hand, "let me introduce you to Esther. Esther was Ramon's nurse when he was in the Joh'burg hospital. I talked her into spending the weekend with us."

For Max it was love at first sight. He felt as though he had been hit by a lightning bolt between the eyes. Esther looked at this slightly paunchy, definitely-not-Clark-Gable, but more-Ernest-Borgnine man, and felt apprehensive. She held out her hand in greeting and Max took it in both of his.

Three months later they were married.

"With all your hard work to get Max to look respectable, he still looked sloppy," Esther laughed at Carol and Felix after they had returned from their honeymoon. "When he walked into that room, he stopped dead in his tracks. His mouth opened, and when you, Carol, introduced us, he slobbered. He actually slobbered. I couldn't believe it."

"But I had fallen for you," Max said, putting his arm around her. "You looked so beautiful I could not even think of something clever to say."

She kissed him on his cheek. "Well darling, your performance at the dinner table after a few glasses of wine made up for everything. I think that is when I fell in love with you."

Max grunted.

"I have never laughed so much or enjoyed myself as much as I did that evening. Do you know," she confided to them, "that when Max proposed on Sunday afternoon, I never took him seriously. I thought he was joking, but when he offered to drive me back to Johannesburg, that was when I realized that he was serious. On Monday he bought the ring, and on Tuesday talked me into accepting it. I still can't believe that everything went so quickly."

"What was the point of waiting?" Max chipped in. "We knew that we were perfect for each other. Why delay the inevitable?"

"You may have known, but I was still in doubt," Esther teased, trying not to laugh. "It was only when we stood under the chupah [bridal canopy], that I began to question as to whether I had made the right decision."

"I had to move fast," Max teased her, "I was so scared you would change your mind. I had to tie the knot quickly, before you had a chance to reconsider."

She kissed him, long and hard. "I made an excellent choice," she said. "As match-makers," she said to Carol, "you and Felix have won many paths to paradise."

They lived in the old house Dasser had built for his wife Janie, when he had brought her to Brakenstroom, but Esther wanted something more modern, so they sold the house and bought one, in exactly in the style she wanted, with a swimming pool and a beautiful garden. That was when Max found out that he had no money. It had been easy for a bachelor to live off produce given by grateful patients in lieu of a bill, but food did not buy clothes, nor could it support a family, and Esther wanted to start a family before she became too old. For the first time in his practice, he started charging his patients regularly. Esther managed his books, sending out the necessary accounts, but habits are hard to change, and she still found that her kitchen had more vegetables and fruit than they had money in the bank. Also, feeding chickens cost money, and a slice of roast beef every now and then would have been a welcome change from the diet of fried, boiled, roasted, curried, and even pickled chicken.

Eventually, fate played its hand. Ten miles outside Brakenstroom, the South African Government had years before built a mental hospital for the severely retarded. The hospital was part of a huge farming complex, and those patients that were able to work obtained therapy by working in the fields. The majority of patients had no chance of ever recovering mentally. These patients were, in many cases, forgotten by their families; patients who had to be cared for twenty-four hours a day; patients who existed simply to die. They were the genetically handicapped, deformed, and retarded. The name of the institution was Helderand, named after the low range of small hills on which it was built.

Helderand provided the citizens of Brakenstroom with employment, and besides all the nurses and nurses' aides who worked there, it also employed six psychiatrists and two medical doctors. It was a teaching institution, with a continuous stream of young budding students in the medical and nursing fields from Universities around the country, who in their final year would learn about the worst mental cases in South Africa.

The position of Superintendent fell vacant. After a great deal of consideration and with a lot of heartache, Max and Esther decided that he should sell his practice and apply for the position. They could no longer afford to live on barter. Working for the government, Max would receive a steady monthly salary, which although not fantastic, would at least give him a living wage. Also, there was the attraction of a pension and other fringe benefits that came with the position.

He sent in his application, was called for the first interview and three months later was appointed to the position. He advertised his practice and sold it to a young doctor at a good price. Max had never been so financially secure in his life, but it was with a heavy heart that he bade each patient farewell.

His new position as superintendent involved a great deal of administrative work, but with his usual charm and complete lack of business acumen, he soon delegated all the work to those staff who had been administering the institution very efficiently all along.

He started spending more and more time in the clinic and very soon was back into his love as a general practitioner, treating his new patients with the same devotion that he had given his patients when he was in private practice.

Max was happy and so was Esther. She socialized with the local community and kept herself busy with charitable work. She was pregnant, enjoying the subtle changes to her body, something she had always nursed in others. She had never ever imagined that she could be so happy.

One of Max's self-inflicted duties was ward rounds. With two doctors and a psychiatrist in tow, he would visit each ward at least once a week, familiarizing himself with each patient, but it was the children's ward that continually broke his heart. He would often ask Esther rhetorically, "How is it that these little mites will have to spend their whole lives in an institution? What is their purpose in His Divine Plan? Surely He should cure them?" And he would shake his head in frustration.

He started spending more and more time in the children's ward, gradually becoming involved with each child personally, pestering the psychiatrists with questions as to treatment and results obtained.

"There must be a way we can help them lead better lives," he would ask, over and over again.

The children started recognizing him, and his tremendous empathy for them often broke through their mental barriers. One child, whom the staff called Tzippie, started to follow him on his rounds, telling him about each patient. She acted as his interpreter, and it was as though she had a personal relationship with each one.

"Uncle," she would say in Afrikaans. She was Afrikaans-speaking, and this was the polite way to address him. "Uncle, Bertie says he wants a sweet."

Bertie sat curled in the corner of his cot as usual, oblivious to all around him. Max would look at him closely for some sign of recognition or movement. He had started carrying a handful of barley sugar sweets in his pocket, and if a child behaved while he examined them, he always gave them one, as a "thank-you."

"How do you know?" he asked Tzippie, puzzled. He had seen no sign of any movement from Bertie.

"He told me," she would explain, and then he marveled at the way a child who was catatonic would suddenly stretch out a hand to take the sweet from Tzippie's fingers, popping it into his mouth.

This happened often, and soon without being consciously aware of it, he became dependent on Tzippie when he went on his ward rounds. He never questioned the fact that she was always there, friendly with each and every patient and staff member. She always wore the same dress, well-washed and faded, and she was always barefoot. Occasionally, she would have a ribbon in her hair, and once she even wore a pair of dirty white takkies (sneakers), but she soon took them off. She was small, and looked about four years old. He never thought much about it.

"If Tzippie can get through to them," he admonished his staff one day at a monthly meeting, "why can't we?"

"Who is Tzippie?" one of the newer psychiatrists asked.

"Tzippie is one of the patients of ward six, the pediatric ward." said Dr. Grobler, a psychiatrist Max had difficulty in befriending. For some reason, he didn't like Max, and he showed it in his abrupt attitude and unfriendly behaviour. Max had decided that he was either anti-semitic, or that he had most probably applied for the position of superintendent, and having lost it to Max, showed his antagonism by being unco-operative.

Max looked up from his desk where he was sitting. All those present at the meeting sat in a semi-circle around the front of the desk. Dr. Grobler had stood up as he spoke and moved towards the window on Max's left.

"What do you mean, patient?" Max looked puzzled. "Isn't she one of the nursing staff's children?"

Grobler laughed sardonically, unable to hide his dislike for Max. "No staff member may, or would, even dream of bringing their children here," he declared contemptuously. "I am surprised that you could even think that someone would." He walked to the window and, turning his back on everybody, looked out into the gardens.

Max reddened. Grobler was right.

"Tzippie is a patient, all right." Grobler continued without turning to look at them. "Perhaps it is because she has grown up amongst these children that she makes them react positively to her." He gestured to the window. "Take a look."

Max stood up and walked to the window, as did the others. Tzippie was wheeling a wheelchair through the gardens. She was jabbering continually and her face was alive with her conversation. The patient kept moving his head wherever she pointed, and occasionally laughed with her. They could not hear what she said, but the picture was a very happy one. Max looked closer at the patient. He recognized Bertie.

"But there is nothing wrong with her," Max blurted out. "Anyone can see that."

They turned to look at him, and slowly took their seats. Grobler remained standing at the window, watching the two children playing in the garden.

"There **is** absolutely nothing wrong with her," he snapped, "even as far as you can't see either," he turned to look at Max, "except perhaps that she is a little small for her age."

"How old is she? " Max asked, leaning forward.

"She has been here almost seven years," Grobler retorted, "which means that she is almost seven."

"She has been here since birth?" Max was amazed. "Then she must be retarded. She looks about four or five. Something must be wrong with her. Why else would she be here?"

Grobler coughed, reddened slightly, and replied angrily, stressing each word as he spoke. "Do you always make rash decisions in areas you know very little about?" He said loudly, "Man, this child should be in school, and if she were, she would be top of her class. I cannot even determine what her . . ." Then, as though realizing he may be saying more than he wanted to, he stopped and controlled himself.

"Did you examine her?" he asked Max, his voice trembling with his anger. "If you have, did you find her retarded? And if you did not examine her, as I assume you didn't because you simply think that she is one of the staff's children, then obviously as far as your off-the-cuff diagnosis is concerned, she isn't retarded. You said so yourself a few minutes ago." He was so angry that he was almost incoherent. He had walked toward the desk as he spoke and leaned forward, his face close to Max's, his knuckles white where they supported his weight on the desk, a sharp contrast to his face, which was blood-red with anger.

Max was shocked. The venom that emanated from Dr. Grobler was all directed at him. He looked down at the drops of spittle on the desk that had flown from Grobler's mouth as he punctuated each word. Grobler's face strained as he struggled to control his anger. Max looked up at the furious face a few inches from his own. A vein was throbbing in Grobler's temple. He half stood up from his chair, anticipating a further burst of vehemence, but Grobler leaned back from the desk, and with difficulty brought his anger under control. Max sat back in his chair.

"You are right," he muttered so softly that only Grobler heard him. "I did not. I never ever considered that she might be one of the patients, in fact I never even queried her presence here. Yes, you are right about her intelligence. I would go so far as to say that she could be very much above average."

"She *is* above average," Grobler said quietly, punctuating each word with a finger on Max's desk. " She is so bloody far above average that I cannot find an upper limit to her I.Q."

"You gave her an I.Q. test?" one of the psychiatrists charged. "Which one?"

"The tests are in the outer office," Grobler brushed off the question. "Go look for yourself."

"Then what is she doing here?" one of the doctors asked. "Surely there must be something wrong with her?"

Grobler turned to look at the questioner. "Jan," he said coldly, "I have examined her thoroughly and found her to be an extremely healthy child. I know that she is above average intelligence, although she is still too young to undergo a proper test. Man, this child has been reading ever since she was three years old, and that is what made me decide to try and find out just how clever she really is."

He walked around the room as he spoke, agitated at being questioned. He stopped at the window, and again looked out into the garden.

"At first I thought that she may be a savant," he said and turned to look at Max as he spoke. Max sat white-faced in his chair, his hands a pyramid in front of his nose and mouth, as he absorbed everything Grobler said. "But I found that she was simply a little girl, and a very captivating little girl at that. In fact, I have even taken her home with me most weekends. My wife and my children adore her. You cannot believe the effect she has on people."

"Why hasn't she been sent home then?" Max asked quietly, in control of his emotions once more. "Surely her parents ought to be notified?"

Grobler did not answer immediately. He turned slowly and looked at them all as they waited for his answer.

"I have written to her parents a number of times," he explained, "but they reply that their child was declared brain-damaged at birth, and they refuse to believe that she is normal. They feel it is better for her and for them, of course, if she should spend her life in this institution."

"Who committed her?"

Grobler turned to the questioner, searched the man's face and looked out the window once more at the two figures still playing on the grass. Then he looked at Max.

"Doctor," he growled, "you will have to excuse me. I have a patient who needs me urgently," and without waiting for Max to acknowledge him, he walked to the door, hesitated and turned back to look at Max. In a voice that was almost inaudible but filled with emotion, he said, "I would suggest that you read her file." He walked out of the office, bumping into the doorway, drunk with anger.

The meeting broke up noisily, with everybody talking about Grobler's outburst. Some of them were surprised because it was unlike Grobler to become emotionally involved with a patient. They all gradually left Max's office, taking one last look out the window, but Tzippie and Bertie were no longer there.

Max sat at his desk, trembling and very upset. Dr. Grobler was a very good psychiatrist, but he felt the anger that had been unleashed at him during the meeting was unnecessary. He realized that sooner than later he and Grobler would have to have a showdown. It could no longer be avoided.

Later that morning, on his way to his rounds, he asked his secretary to put Tzippie's file in his briefcase.

"I would like to read it tonight, at home," he countered, when she nervously asked why he wanted it.

"I don't think it is here," she avoided his gaze. "I think . . . I think . . . ." She had heard the shouting in Max's office earlier that morning; almost everyone in the reception room had heard it. Every doctor that walked out of the room had asked for Tzippie's file, but she did not know where it was. She looked at Max, her eyes wide with apprehension, her bottom lip quivering.

"What do you mean, it's not here?" he shouted at her. "Find it. Someone must have it and I want it."

"Yes, Doctor," she answered, and burst into tears.

Max stomped off, angry with himself for having shouted at his secretary, and annoyed that any file should go missing, especially this one.

Tzippie was waiting for him at the entrance to the ward. As he approached, her face lit up with a smile. This time, though, he carefully noted everything about her. Her shabby dress was faded blue today, with a white floral pattern. The matching blue bow in her combed brown hair, hair that had been cut page-boy style by Helderand's barber, was not at all stylish or practical. Her hair was naturally curly, something the barber missed when he wet it to cut the ends to the same length. Her eyes were green and crystal clear without a blemish, and her nose had a sprinkling of freckles at the bridge. As always, she was barefoot with toes that splayed slightly, free from the restriction of shoes. She skipped towards him and slipped her small hand in his.

"Oh, Uncle," she said in Afrikaans, "I am so glad you are here. Susanne says she has stomach ache, and it hurts very much, and Paul," she pronounced the name the Afrikaans way, 'Pole' "says that . . ."

He knelt down, and, holding her by her shoulders, studied her carefully. She stopped talking and looked at him, holding his gaze as though she queried his scrutiny. Then her eyes crinkled with a smile, her cheeks dimpling as she tilted her head to her left.

"Tzippie," he asked her very seriously, interrupting her as she continued telling him about the children in the ward, "how old are you?"

"Oh!" she exclaimed, as though surprised by his question. "I am seven, Uncle, and very nearly eight, but come quickly, we must go to Susanne. She is very sick and she only wants to see you."

"Susanne can wait a few more minutes," he said, holding her by her arms. He was still kneeling, and held her firmly before him so that she couldn't run ahead of him to the ward.

"When is your birthday?"

She dimpled. "February twenty-fourth," she answered, "but it is still a long time to my birthday. Auntie Gerda told me that she would give me a party this year, just like the one she gave me last year." She paused, then added. "You can come if you want to."

"Who is Auntie Gerda?" Max was puzzled.

"Auntie Gerda?" Tzippie looked at him, surprised that he should ask. "Why, Auntie Gerda is Sister van der Merwe."

He held her for a few more minutes and felt her squirm in his hands as she became restless. Then he said, as cheerfully as he could, "Thank you for the invitation Tzippie, I accept, but tell me, one last thing . . . who is your Mommy and your Daddy?"

The smile left her face. He was taken aback by the tremendous hurt he saw in her eyes and he was sorry that he had asked, but he had to know if she knew. He waited for her answer. When she did not reply immediately, he asked her again, but more gently.

"Tzippie, do you know who your Mommy and your Daddy are?"

"My Mommy doesn't want me, and my Daddy also does not want me," she answered hesitantly. A sob caught in her throat. She looked around desperately, as though looking for a way to escape her tormentor, and finding none, she moved into his arms and put her head against his chest. He stroked her hair and felt her tears as they soaked through his shirt. After a few minutes she pulled away, sighed deeply, and then laughed. "Why, you are all my family," she shouted, and she stretched her arms out to embrace everything around her. "Everyone here is my Mommy and my Daddy, and I love you all." She threw her arms around his neck and kissed him on his cheek. Max was so surprised at this gesture that he nearly fell backwards and had to put both his arms around her, to save himself from falling. For almost a full minute he knelt with her in his arms, feeling her small trembling body, and a wave of emotion came over him, such as he had never before experienced.

It was Tzippie who shook herself free of his grasp. She took his hand.

"But come now," she urged him determinedly, "we must go to Susanne."

He stood up slowly, trying to regain his composure and followed her, her hand in his. He was confused and slightly bewildered about his feelings towards her. She had mentally seduced him, he realized. He was totally captivated by her, and he marveled at the way she had turned a tense emotional situation, one that he had created, into something that she could handle. She had been the adult, not he.

He listened to her as she translated Susanne's thoughts while he examined the sick child, but now, instead of simply accepting her ability as something natural and commonplace, he mentally queried every aspect of it. He watched her actions closely, the way she communicated with Susanne, a child who never ever spoke.

When he returned to his office, Tzippie's file lay on his desk. It was very thick, held together by a broad elastic band, and the dog-ears on the cover showed that it had been used often. It was late, and he and Esther were going out for the evening, so he put it into his briefcase and went home.

That night, as they lay in bed, he told Esther about the meeting in his office. "I still don't know why Grobler was so angry. There is no doubt in my mind that the child does not belong in the institution. You know, I have become extremely fond of her. Somehow, she just gets to you."

"It looks as though I have competition," Esther laughed, "but then of course I should easily be able to outwit a seven-year-old and regain my husband's affections."

"This is no seven-year-old." Max muttered. "She is more like a wise old woman in the body of a seven-year-old. It is incredible how she handles adversity. Wait until you meet her." He lay back on the cushions and looked up at the ceiling. "I found today's events quiet unsettling," he told her as he played the events of the day over in his mind. "Grobler's outburst was probably justified, but he was so vehement in it. I mean, if the child is normal, then send her home. Why all the anger?"

Esther looked up from the book she was reading. She had never known Max so agitated.

He got out of bed.

"Where are you going?" Esther asked.

"I want to look over Tzippie's file," he said. "The whole case worries me."

He took the file from his briefcase, and removed the elastic band. He read the name on the front cover.

"Tzipporah Lewis," he read. "Tzippie's name is Tzipporah," he murmured softly.

"Why," Esther answered, closing her book, "with a Hebrew

name like Tzipporah, and a surname like Lewis, she could very well be Jewish."

Max went white.

"Esther . . . my God, it can't be," he almost choked.

Esther looked at him, frightened by what she saw in his face. "Max," she cried sitting upright in bed. "What's wrong, what is *wrong*?"

Max sat with the unopened file in his hand. "Esther," he repeated, his voice a monotone of emotion, "I was the one who delivered Tzippie. I was the one who had her committed. I remember it all, but . . . but . . . I don't believe that my diagnosis could have been so wrong." He sat with the file on his lap, trying to remember everything that had happened seven years ago when he delivered Esme Lewis's baby.

He opened the file and started reading aloud about a baby, almost lifeless, with a deformed skull, who had been brought into the institution by a nurse from the Brakenstroom Hospital. No one had expected the child to live, but the little thing had clung to life with a determination that had surprised everyone. As the days passed, the staff had begun to wonder at this, and had silently cheered her on. Her skull started rounding, and when, after almost seven weeks of lying absolutely still with eyes closed, totally helpless, she started moving first one leg, then the other, they had all celebrated. The nurse on duty had written how they had rushed to her cradle, to wonder at this miracle.

"It had taken almost eight months for her skull to fill out completely," he said, "and after that, it was simply time and love that had healed her. At first they all thought she would be spastic, and badly at that, but as the months passed, every day saw another part of her body slowly come back to life."

He looked at Esther, expecting her to say something. She sat deep in thought. He continued reading.

"She became a favourite of the physiotherapists," he told her, "and from the reports written it looks like they competed with each other in coaxing a different muscle back to life." He turned the page. "There is a note by Doctor Grobler. He writes that he could only surmise that the child's brain had been badly bruised at birth, and that with time, each brain cell had healed itself."

"This is a case of Nature being the Master Physician," Esther said. "What actually happened, Max?" she coaxed, not wanting to upset him.

He told her, at first hesitantly, but as the memories came flooding back, he spoke faster, as though by telling her he would expunge the terrible guilt he felt. "I had forgotten about the baby," he whispered. "I became so busy in my practice, that soon afterwards, I forgot. I had no idea . . ." and he buried his face in his hands. "Jerry and Esme moved to Durban soon afterwards, and I thought that they took the baby with them."

Esther took the file from him.

"It looks as though Dr. Grobler has been rather busy," she murmured.

Max dropped his hands from his face. "What do you mean?" he asked, looking at her curiously.

"Well," Esther said, "there are a number of letters where he has written to the Lewis's, telling them that their child was normal, and that they should come and fetch her. There is even a letter from Jerry saying that Dr. Grobler must be mistaken. Max, you must read this. It's unbelievable that a father could be so callous." She held out the letter to him.

He took it from her, and wiped away his tears with the sleeve of his pajama top. He read where Jerry had replied to Grobler that Esme had suffered tremendously when she had been told that her child was "stillborn," and that she would not be able to have another. He had no desire to introduce her at this time in her life to a "mentally retarded infant," and have to tell her, "this is your dead child come back to life."

Max looked at the date on the letter. It was dated just over two years ago. "Surely," he said, "I could have been informed of the change in the child." He took the file from Esther. She watched his face carefully as he paged rapidly through it. He found what he was looking for, a letter addressed to him, but it had been returned "address unknown." The address on the envelope had the town as Durban, and not Brakenstroom. The person who typed the envelope must have assumed that he lived in the same city as the Lewis's.

He lay back in bed, put both hands behind his head and studied the ceiling. After a few minutes he turned to Esther who had been monitoring his thoughts as they expressed themselves on his face. Then he smiled.

"My dear, how would you like to help me bring a family together again?"

"I would love to," she replied, curious as to his intentions. "What nefarious scheme do you have in mind?"

"Well, let us start by . . ." They put their heads together and planned late into the night.

The next day, he arranged for Tzippie to live with them. He called Dr. Grobler and those members of the staff whom he felt were interested in Tzippie's welfare, to his office, where he explained his plan to them.

"It is my intention to reunite her with her parents," he declared. "To achieve this she has to be taught how to speak English. Her parents are English-speaking and not only that, the Lewis's are also Jewish, which is why she should live with my wife and I. I will take her out of the institution today. I know that I must have her father's permission to do this, but I hope that you will all support me in what I intend to do, without getting this permission."

"As long as you bring her back to visit us," Sister van der Merwe demanded. "You know she is our child. We all breathed life into the lifeless doll that was left at our doorstep. One could say that she was she was born here, and we were all present at her birth."

"I realize that, and I will be forever grateful to all of you for correcting a wrong I made," Max said humbly, "but it is now time to take the next step. She should be with her natural parents. She is also six, correction, nearly seven and she should be receiving a proper education. I have already arranged with Smut's Primary and they have agreed to accept her." Smut's Primary was the local English-speaking school.

"Dr. Asher," Grobler growled, "I have possibly misjudged you. You have my full support." He held out his hand to Max. "But remember," he continued, "we will be watching you."

Max looked at the outstretched hand, pleased that it was there, and took it, gripping it firmly. He smiled as Grobler smiled, relieved that a probable enemy was now a possible friend. This man had tried so hard to get the Lewis's to take Tzippie, and he had failed. It was now Max's turn. He couldn't afford to fail. He now knew Tzippie's file intimately and if Grobler had at any time condemned Max for committing her, his outstretched hand was a sign of forgiveness.

"Thank you," Max said, looking at him gratefully. "Thank you, all of you."

Later that morning, Esther came to fetch Tzippie.

"But where are you taking me?" she asked Esther in Afrikaans, not understanding what was happening.

"You are coming to live with us for a while," Esther said gently, so as not to frighten her.

"But why?" she asked, confused. "This is my home. All my friends are here."

"You have to go to school, Tzippie, wouldn't you like that?" Esther asked.

"Oh yes," Tzippie replied, her face lighting up, "I would like that very much, but why now, why this sudden change?" She looked at Esther quizzically.

Esther thought quickly, "Because you are a growing girl," she answered, "and all children who grow should attend school."

Tzippie digested her answer, and then accepting what Esther had told her, spun on her heel and ran from Max's office. "I must tell everyone that I am going to school," she shouted as she ran into Sister van der Merwe's legs. "Auntie Gerda," she shouted, "I am going to school. I must tell Bertie," and she ran to the wards.

"Bertie said that he will miss me," she said in the car as they drove through the gates of Helderand. "I also told Susanne that she will have to get better, so that she can come to school with me . . ." She chattered away with excitement as Esther drove, talking non-stop for the whole journey to her new home.

That night, Max hardly recognized her. Her hair had been stylishly cut, she wore a new dress with matching shoes, which she kept taking off, and she couldn't stop talking, she was so excited.

"I bought her everything she needed," Esther said to him, kissing him as he walked in the door. "You can't imagine how exhausting this shopping expedition was, but she is absolutely delightful. Wherever I took her she simply charmed everyone."

"Well," Max smiled as he looked at Tzippie, "what a difference a proper hair style and some decent clothes can do. Now comes the hard part. We start playing Pygmalion."

Tzippie started school the next day. She did not have much trouble learning English, but her accent was atrocious and when she became angry, she slipped into Afrikaans. Esther took her for elocution lessons and she loved them, especially where she had to play act.

Everyone that taught her was amazed at how quickly she was able to learn, and she soon became 'teacher's pet' in all the classes she attended. She made friends quickly, and Esther found that the constant stream of friends she brought home became tiring, especially as her pregnancy developed, but she did not discourage her.

"There is no doubt about it," Esther reported to Max after a few weeks, "she has an extremely high I.Q. Even Mrs. Conradie, her teacher, remarked today when I fetched her from school, about how clever she is. She is also very popular with the other kids in the class, and apparently simply walks into Koos's office at break to talk with him. There are no flies on her." Koos was the principal of the school, and he was just as intrigued with Tzippie as was everyone else. Max had told him enough of Tzippie's history to have Koos encourage her, and take a special interest in her.

Tzippie insisted on visiting her friends at Helderand once a week. She spent hours with them playing, passing their wants on to Sister van der Merwe and to Max. She still spent the occasional weekend with the Grobler family, and after every visit he would say to Max. "Remarkable child this, remarkable. I always knew she was, but she continues to amaze me."

Five months passed and it was difficult to recognize her as the child that was a "Helderand Orphan." Esther went into labour and Louis was born. Tzippie now had a baby brother whom she doted on. He was a very contented baby, and with Tzippie virtually anticipating his every need, Esther almost felt unneeded.

"Quite honestly," she complained to Max one night, "I thank God Tzippie doesn't have breasts yet. If she had, she may even take away the pleasure of feeding Louis from me." They both laughed. "I don't know how she does it," Esther continued shaking her head. "She simply knows what Louis wants. I know it sounds stupid of me to say this, but it is as though they are communicating with each other."

"That is exactly what happened in the wards," Max replied. "We couldn't get over the fact that she knew what all those kids wanted and needed. I must say that doing a ward round without her is sheer hell. It takes twice as long as before."

Approximately eight months later as they lay in bed, Max said to Esther, "You know, darling, it is time we contacted the Lewis's."

Esther said nothing. Max thought that she had not heard him. "Esther," he repeated, "it is time we contacted the Lewis's."

"I heard you the first time," Esther murmured. "I have been dreading the day you would say that. Isn't it still too early?" she pleaded. "She is only just beginning to speak English without her Afrikaans accent."

"Esther," Max said firmly, "it must be now. We are becoming too fond of her, and the longer we wait, the more difficult it will be to let her go. Even I am beginning to wish that she was ours."

Esther turned her head aside. She did not want Max to see the tears in her eyes.

"You say that so easily," she said dejectedly, "but I suppose you are right. I will miss her terribly." She felt that Tzippie was already her daughter, as much a part of her as was Louis. "What do you suggest we do?" she whispered.

He took her in his arms. "How about a week in Durban? And because we can't find accommodation . . . "

"We will have to stay with Jerry and Esme," she finished for him. "Won't they think it strange, though? You haven't seen them for years. They don't even know me, and here you arrive with a wife and two children. Won't they think it's chutzpah on your part?" She was trying everything to delay his decision.

"Well," Max said softly, understanding the reasons for her argument, "let us find out." He kissed her on the forehead and held her tightly.

"I have a week's holiday owing to me," he said after a few minutes, "and there is nothing like the present to take it up."

The day before they had left for Durban, Max took Tzippie to Helderand. "Tzippie," he said as they walked from the car, "I want you to say goodbye to all your friends, a long goodbye." She stopped and looked up at him, puzzled. "Why, Uncle Max?" she asked, a frown on her face. He knelt so that he could watch her eyes as he spoke. "Well because," he answered, "we are going away for a long time."

She stood before him, searching his face for some sign as to his intentions. He had to look away. She put her hand out and stroked his cheek, and then slowly let her eyes drift over the building behind him, the building that had been her home for so many years.

"Uncle Max," she eventually asked, "Are you taking me to my Mommy?" She looked at him, and he could see her eyes reddening.

"What do you mean, Tzippie ?" he asked, not sure he had heard her question properly.

"Are you taking me home, to my Mommy and Daddy?"

He was amazed at her perception. Surely she must have overheard Esther and him talking. "Why do you think that?" he asked hesitantly, scared to give her a positive "Yes" in case Jerry and Esme rejected her.

"Because . . . because it feels like it," she replied, trying to explain how she knew. "I know that I have a Mommy and Daddy somewhere, and I know that although they don't love me now, they will love me soon, but . . . but . . ." and she started sobbing uncontrollably. He took her in his arms and held her tightly, stroking her hair as she cried. Taking a handkerchief from his pocket, he dabbed at her face, drying her tears.

"You do have a Mommy and a Daddy," he said soothingly. "They have to meet you, and then they will love you, just like Esther and I and everyone else at Helderand loves you."

With eyes red from crying, she looked at the building before her. Reminiscent of the years she had spent there, she said in Afrikaans, "This is my home Uncle Max ,and I love it, and I love everyone who lives in it. This is where I was born. I will never forget this home." Then she said in English, showing a grasp of the situation far in advance of her age,"You and Auntie Esther have taught me that it is time for me to leave. I will say goodbye to everyone here. I will miss them, but it is better. I must go home now." She sighed. "You are right, it is time to go to my Mommy. I have always known that I would have to some day. Somehow, I know she needs me." She let go of his hand and walked through the front door, sniffling, leaving him kneeling in the drive-way watching her.

"I couldn't believe it," he told Esther later that evening. "She grasped the situation and understood without me having to tell her. That day in my office, when Grobler said that he thought she may be a savant, he could have been right, but possibly she is a savant in a way we haven't yet discovered."

"Have you ever considered that she may be an empath?" Esther asked. "You know, one of those people who feel what others are thinking. Psychics have that gift. Tzippie could have a similar type of gift."

"You could be right," Max mused. "I simply find it incredible that one minute she is a child, and the next . . . well, her ability to grasp and understand a situation absolutely astonishes me."

That night they phoned the Lewis's and virtually invited themselves to stay for the week. Jerry was at first taken aback at Max's insistence, but on consideration, he became delighted at the thought of renewing an old friendship.

"Oh, by the way," Max added almost as an afterthought, "we are four. We are bringing a little girl with us. She has never seen the sea and Esther and I made her a promise."

"Girl?" Esme asked after Jerry had hung up the phone and told her about Max and Esther's intended visit. "Unusual, don't you think?"

"It doesn't surprise me at all," Jerry replied casually. "You know Max, he always becomes so involved with his patients. I suppose she is the daughter of one of them. The day he starts charging them is the day they will leave him." He did not know that Max was no longer in private practice. "It will be good to see him again," Jerry continued. "I have heard that Esther, his wife, is absolutely charming. I wonder though . . ."

"You wonder what?" Esme asked.

"No, nothing darling," Jerry muttered, "I just find it strange that after all these years . . ." and he walked from the room without finishing his sentence.

It took two days to drive to Durban, a trip that usually took eight hours. Tzippie had never seen mountains, so they stayed two nights at the Cathedral Peak hotel in the Drakensburg. It was Tzippie's holiday and their enjoyment came from watching her delight in their journey.

They drove to Durban, arriving late in the afternoon. The sea breeze was warm and balmy and the sub-tropical climate of Durban with its luscious vegetation was a stark contrast to the dry Transvaal. Max drove to the beach and they all got out of the car to stretch their legs on the white sand. It was the first time Tzippie had ever seen the sea, and she ran along the sand to the water's edge, shrieking with delight as the waves crashed at her feet.

"Smell it, Auntie Esther," she shouted at them, her voice drowned by the crashing of the surf. She turned her nose into the wind and breathed in deeply. "It smells so different." She laughed and screamed with delight and coaxed them into paddling in the water with her. She insisted that Louis wet his feet and that he feel the wet sand curl between his toes. Eventually she tired and the three of them sat in the sand, with Louis in Esther's arms, each lost in thought, idly watching the waves as they swept in towards them in a continual cycle of motion. Tzippie sat between them enjoying their closeness. She felt their sadness and she shuddered and slipped her hand into Esther's, leaning her head on her shoulder. Esther put her arm around Tzippie and hugged her.

"You are cold," she said. "Let me get you a jersey."

"Uh-uh, no," Tzippie shook her head, snuggling closer to Esther, enjoying her body warmth. "I like the feel of the sea."

"Tzippie," Max said gently after a while. "We have to tell you a story."

Esther looked at him, concern showing in her eyes. "Now?" she mouthed.

"Yes, now,"he nodded.

He told Tzippie the story of her birth, how she had been born with a misshapen skull, and how he had had her committed to Helderand. He told her how God had made her better, but that it had taken a long time, even for Him, to make her well. Jerry, he explained tenderly, was her father and Esme her mother. "Although Jerry, your father, knows about you," Max continued, watching Tzippie's face carefully, "he thinks that you are like Bertie, mentally retarded. Esme, your mother, thinks you died when you were born," he continued cautiously, scared that he would hurt her more than he wanted to. He watched her facial expressions, looking for some sign or movement to indicate her feelings.

She sat for a long time taking it all in, her face expressionless. When he mentioned Esme, she snuggled closer to Esther, who hugged her tighter than ever, scared of the responsibility they were passing on to her.

After what seemed like an eternity, Tzippie asked.

"Do I have any brothers or sisters?"

"No," Max answered cautiously. He looked at Esther as though asking why Tzippie should have known to ask that question. Esther pointed to Louis lying in her lap.

"Esme can't have any more babies," Esther said softly. "When you were born, something went wrong, and she had to have an operation."

Tzippie sat digesting what she had heard. She stroked Louis's head, allowed her hand to fall to his, then leaned over and kissed him. Then she whispered so softly that they almost didn't hear her.

"Then I suppose I will have to go to them." Her voice fell as though she regretted her decision, and then as an afterthought she asked in a very small voice. "What happens if they don't want me?"

"They *will* want you, my darling," Esther assured her, drawing her close. "Everybody wants you, and they will be no exception."

"Yes," Tzippie murmured in a small voice, still not assured. Then looking up at Esther she pleaded, "But what would happen if I find that I don't love them?"

Esther and Max said nothing. Tzippie continued, her voice rising with emotion. "My Daddy didn't want me. My Mommy thinks I am dead. Do you really want me to go to them?" There was a sob in her voice.

"Oh my darling," Esther whispered desperately and hugged her closer. "We want you. We love you so much, I wish you would stay with us always, but you must first see your real mother. If you don't want to stay with her, then you can come home to us."

"We promise you that, Tzipporah," Max said.

Tzippie broke out of Esther's hug and stood up. She turned to face them, then frowned and looked down at the wet sand where her one foot had traced an abstract pattern. She looked up at Esther intently and saw the tears in her eyes. Max gave her an awkward smile, not knowing what to do.

"Promise me," she cried out in Afrikaans, "promise me that if I don't like them, if they don't want me, that you will take me home with you. That you won't make me stay with them." The fact that she spoke in Afrikaans told them how upset she was. She looked so frail standing before them, the wind tugging at her hair and her dress. Esther looked at Max with relief and he at her. Then they both laughed, "Any time," they shouted in unison.

"You promise?" Tzippie asked, not understanding their behaviour.

"Yes, my darling, we promise." All the love Esther felt for Tzippie showed in her words. Reaching for her, she took her in her arms, and kissed her and hugged her. "How anyone can resist you, though, would surprise me."

It was not until the third day that Jerry asked Max about Tzippie. They were relaxing on the verandah overlooking the beach. The sun was setting over the sea as screaming gulls pestered the fisherman. Max sat sipping a Laphroig Malt that Jerry had introduced him to.

"She is our daughter, isn't she?" Jerry asked, not looking at Max.

Max held his glass up to the light. He looked at the setting sun through the amber liquid, sipped a little and rolled it around his tongue, enjoying the flavor of a pure malt whisky. Then he answered. "Yes."

"But how could you do this to me," Jerry said angrily, turning to him. "You could have told me . . . before you came."

"No," Max answered, interrupting him. "You have the question wrong. How could *you* have done this to her? And we did tell you. Dr. Grobler wrote to you three times, and you could not even be bothered to come and see your own child."

Jerry sat for a long time, silent. Max could see the torment in his friend's face, and felt justified in letting him suffer. "But you committed her," Jerry grimaced. "You saw what she looked like when she was born. You said that she would be brain damaged. How could you have made such a mistake?"

Max raised his glass to his lips and drank deeply, the alcohol burning his tongue. He stood up and walked to the edge of the verandah. It was always so easy to cast blame. He turned wearily to face Jerry.

"Yes," he said through clenched teeth. "I committed her and I have tortured myself with that guilt from the day I found her. Hell, man, doctors aren't omnipotent. We are human, we make mistakes, and we suffer for them. This was the worst error I have ever made, and I hope that those I make in the future, and let's face it, I will make more mistakes, will not be nearly as bad as this one. I have to live with what I did to Tzipporah, but somehow the Almighty gave me a chance to correct my mistake, and correct it I will. If you don't want her, then Esther and I will take her and by God, I hope you don't want her." He looked angrily at Jerry, as though willing him to give up Tzippie. "It's up to you now," he said quietly, his voice steely with his determination.

Jerry watched Max closely. He saw the anger in his face and regretted his question. "How," he asked dejectedly, "how can I tell Esme the truth?"

"That," Max replied bitingly, "is the mistake *you* made. I made a bad one. You compounded it." He turned his back to Jerry and watched the sun cast one lingering ray towards the dark sea before finally vanishing below the horizon. His anger left him, and he realized the problem that Jerry was now facing.

"What does Esme think of Tzippie ?" he asked, turning to Jerry.

Jerry looked at him with surprise on his face. "Can't you see?" he cried. "Tzipporah has stolen her heart. I see it every day, and it eats me up. Esme is crying for the daughter she never had."

"But she has one now, and you have to tell her that."

"Yes," Jerry groaned, burying his face in his hands. "Yes, but how?"

He looked up as Esme, holding Tzippie's hand, walked into the front garden. Tzippie was chattering away as usual, and Esme was laughing at what she was saying. He looked at Esme's face, and saw a joy and happiness there that he had not seen in her since they were first married.

"It is unbelievable," he said softly, "that this child should have captured Esme's affections so quickly."

It was Tzippie, though, who solved Jerry's problem. Esther had, over the days, quietly withdrawn from all the shopping excursions and trips to the beach, leaving Esme and Tzippie more and more alone together. She had pleaded being tired from looking after Louis, a plan she and Max had worked out if they saw that the two were getting along with each other. It was on one of these shopping trips, while Esme and Tzippie were relaxing in a restaurant, Esme with a cup of tea and Tzippie demolishing an ice cream, that Esme very quietly asked her, "Tzippie?"

Tzippie looked up from her plate. The tone of Esme's voice had instinctively alerted her that Esme's question was important.

"Yes," and then added so softly that she was sure Esme would not hear it, "Mommy?"

Esme went white. Her hands started trembling and she leaned back in her chair. Tzippie watched her reaction and then took her hand, holding it in both of hers.

"You . . . you called me Mom . . . Mommy," Esme stammered.

Tzippie did not reply, but squeezed her hand tightly.

"Are you . . . are you . . . sure?" Esme asked hesitantly.

"Oh yes," Tzippie replied, and then with more finality and conviction, "Yes . . . Mommy. Uncle Max told me that you are my mommy, and I can feel it here." She pointed to her heart.

Esme started crying softly. She sat in her chair, allowing the tears to fall unheeded down her cheeks. All the time, Tzippie watched her closely, looking for some sign of rejection. After a few minutes, Esme took out a tissue, wiped her eyes, and blew her nose. "I suspected it," she murmured. "When Max and Esther insisted on staying with us, and when they said that they were bringing along a little girl, I knew, but I was so scared."

"You thought that I would be like . . . like Bertie?" Tzippie asked, not certain why Esme should have been scared.

Esme sensed that her answer had to be perfect. She was not sure who Bertie was, but felt that he was someone important in Tzippie's life. "Yes, and I have always loved you as soon as I found out about you, even when I believed you were like Bertie. I was scared that they were not bringing you, but somebody else."

It was Tzippie's turn to be confused, "But . . . how did you know about me?" she asked hesitantly. "Uncle Max said . . . he said that . . . that you thought . . . I . . . I was dead."

"Uncle Max doesn't know everything, and Uncle Jerry," and she caught herself, "uhh Jerry . . ."

"You mean Daddy," Tzippie murmured.

"Yes," Esme continued, "Daddy." The name sounded so wonderful to her ears. "Daddy can't hide anything from me for long. I found an account from Helderand. I wondered why he should be paying fees at the institution. When I phoned Helderand out of curiosity, they told me that the account was for a little girl that had been committed. I was confused. I asked how old you were, and when they told me, I knew you were my daughter. Somehow I just knew. The next time I was in Johannesburg, I drove to Helderand. I wanted to see you. I sat outside in my car the whole morning. I just couldn't go inside. I will never forgive myself for that. I could have had you two years ago."

"You came to me two years ago?" Tzippie said, then shook her head. "I couldn't go with you then. Bertie and Susanne needed me. Did you come any other time?"

"I visited you a thousand times," Esme answered. "Every time I was in Johannesburg, I drove to Helderand and sat outside in the car, trying to find the courage to go in and see you. Once, I even sat in the foyer, but . . . I was too scared." She looked at the earnest young face before her. "I was scared that you wouldn't love me because I wasn't there when you needed me. I hadn't been there to help you grow up. I cried that I couldn't hold you, and love you. I was so scared."

Tzippie looked at Esme, her mother, her mascara smudged with tears, blue streaks lining each cheek. Love and anxiety were etched on her face. Tzippie's eyes widened and then she laughed and threw her arms around Esme's neck and kissed her.

"Oh, Mommy," she cried and laughed at the same time, "I love you so much."

That night, at table, after they had all eaten, Tzippie stood up hesitantly at her place. She looked at Esme who nodded.

"Everyone, please listen," Tzippie said, "I have something to say."

Esther and Max put down their dessert spoons and looked at her questioningly. She smiled back at them. Jerry, surprised and feeling very uncomfortable, looked at Esme and tried to catch her eyes, but Esme would not look at him.

"Today," Tzippie said, smiling at Esme, "when I went to town, I found something that I had always looked for and wanted, but could never find." She walked to Esme, kissed her and, putting both arms around her neck, hugged her, all the time carefully watching Jerry's reaction as he sat at the head of the table. His face was white. She reached for and found Esme's hand, and Esme squeezed it with reassurance. "I found my Mommy," she said. Esme put her arm around her, kissed her on the cheek, then gave her a slight push towards Jerry. He sat frozen to his seat, mixed and confused emotions shadowing his face. Esther and Max looked at each other and smiled as Tzippie slowly approached Jerry.

"Have I . . . have I found my Daddy also?" she asked hesitantly.

Max thought Jerry would faint. He was trembling as he watched every move the child made. She moved a little closer to him and asked again, with a tremor in her voice.

"Have I . . . have I found my Daddy?"

Jerry reached out, took her hand, and slowly raised it to his lips. Then he pulled her towards him and hugged her, smothering her with kisses.

"Yes . . . . Yes you have," he said. "Oh yes, and how you have."

Hettie

BRAKENSTROOM, LIKE EVERY OTHER TOWN in South Africa, had its township of blacks, situated on swampy land that no white wanted. This township was called "The Location," the name derived from a "location of blacks," but eventually becoming "The Location," with a capital "T" and a capital "L."

In Brakenstroom, this land was in the south of the town, bordered on the one side by the local garbage dump and on the other by the town's sewage works. The Brak River flowed slowly through the area, and because the land was low and swampy, any rain that was slightly above average caused the river to break its banks, flooding the township.

The river was beautiful and many of the town's folk, in order to justify the misery of The Location, would argue, "But look at them, they have the beautiful river, with beautiful land. They just do not appreciate what we have given them. They pay no taxes and they get the land for free. What more do they want?"

Now you may think a river flowing slowly through your township an asset, especially if the river is lined with graceful willow trees, dipping branches like trailing fingers into the slowly flowing water. To the north of Brakenstroom, yes, it was an asset, with the value of a property that bordered the river double the average price. But south of the town, the swamp bred nothing but mosquitoes, big black ones that left large painful sores where they bit, and small brown ones that at times could blacken the full moon in their swarms.

The combination of swamp and sewage gave The Location a very distinct odour, which the residents became used to, but when the wind blew into the town from the south, the smell reminded many a Brakenstroomer of the Location's squalor. In the cold of winter, that same wind coming off the swamp often ended a black child's life with bronchitis, pleurisy or pneumonia.

The "other side of the tracks," as poor neighbourhoods in any town are often called, also lay along the river, just above the swamp. This was where the poor whites of Brakenstroom lived, separated from the natives by a school for coloureds, a row of blue gum trees, and a pot-holed dusty dirt road.

This was where Hettie, Max's receptionist, was born, one of three girls and four boys. She was born to the misery and poverty that was part and parcel of living in Vlei Straat (Swamp Street). Her grandparents had come to Brakenstroom with the Voortrekkers from the Cape. But after losing their three sons in the Anglo-Boer War, they sold their farm, drifted to the town, and gradually with the help of mampoer (peach brandy) and later skokiaan (a potent brew distilled by the natives), lost their will to live. Hettie's grandmother, aged beyond her years by her sorrow, slowly sold off all their remaining assets to support her husband and daughter. When her grandfather eventually died, probably from alcoholic poisoning, her grandmother soon followed, leaving her daughter with the house on Vlei Street, and not much else.

Hettie's parents were "poor whites," competing in the labour market with the natives, who worked for a pittance. Her father, in between what little work he could find, spent most of his days drunk, lying in his bed, or in the yard, or wherever he crawled to when the sun shone, and in South Africa, the sun shone almost every day. He was a thin, whining man, continually bemoaning his lot and complaining about his health and his half-empty bottle of cheap wine.

"This fucking stuff is the only thing that keeps me alive," he would cough, patting the bottle while smoke curled from the cigarette butt between his nicotine-stained fingers. Yet, beneath this appearance of weakness and ill health, he was still strong enough to beat his wife when she refused his "partaking of a poor man's pleasure."

Whenever he made these demands (which fortunately was not that often, as most times he was too drunk to perform), Hettie would lie cringing in bed, listening to his shouts. From the age of four, which was as far back as she could remember, she would lie in bed sobbing, waiting for Ma, as the children called their mother, to go to the bathroom and nurse her face where she had been beaten. She would crawl out of bed and go to Ma, burying her tear-stained face in Ma's thin nightie and cry softly with her.

"Go back to bed, Hettiejie," Ma would whisper lovingly, stroking her hair as she comforted her, but Hettie would cling to Ma all the more. Eventually, as her sobbing subsided, Ma would lift her tenderly in her arms and carry her back to the bed she shared with her two sisters, Sissie and Corrie. Sissie, the eldest of the girls, had learned to sleep through the noise, while Corrie, the youngest, would lie in bed shivering, too scared to move, waiting for Hettie to return.

"Now, go to sleep," Ma would murmur lovingly into her ear and, giving Hettie a last hug, she would kiss her gently on the forehead and lay her down on the bed.

"Goodnight, my baby," she would whisper to Corrie as Corrie snuggled up to Hettie's body, worming her way into her arms. The two children would lie in bed, eyes tightly closed, listening to Ma as she made her way back to the kitchen. From the hiss of the steaming kettle and the clink of a cup to a saucer, Hettie knew that Ma had made herself a cup of tea. She knew that she would stay there until Gert, her father, had fallen asleep. Then Ma would once more make her way to the bed they shared, looking in at them as she passed their room. Most times, Hettie heard Ma's every movement and pictured her actions from their sound and, when Ma tiptoed into their room Hettie would open her eyes, smile up at her, and whisper, "Goodnight Ma, I love you," and take delight in the smile that appeared on a face that was always in a frown of continual worry.

Sissie looked like their father, very thin and wiry, with enormous eyes covered by thick bushy eyebrows. Her dark brown hair was always drawn back in a bun that accentuated the appearance of severity. She was withdrawn and seldom spoke, but she was a hard worker, helping Ma with the housekeeping and with the sewing that they took in to make ends meet. This was their only source of income, earning enough money every week to buy the small amount of groceries needed to keep starvation from the door.

The boys helped now and then by fishing on the weekends in the Brak River, but they fished more for the sport, preferring to play games under the willow trees than catch a decent-sized fish. When they did have a catch, it was usually Geel Vis (yellow fish), a type of river carp with fine bones that were inclined to catch in one's teeth; or "Modder Vis" (mud fish) that tended to taste of the mud from which it was spawned; or even the whiskered Barbel (catfish), that other fishermen discarded.

Gert, the eldest son, named after his father, was always too busy with his friends to help in the house. He was a rough boy, taller than most boys of his age, and a bad student. He had failed two years in a row at school, and so was the oldest boy in his class. He was a bully who took great delight in swearing at the Jewish boys in his class, never hesitating to start a fight whenever he saw them at the local swimming pool or at the bioscope (cinema) on those few occasions when he was able to obtain a ticket.

"The Jews murdered Christ," he would shout at Max Asher. He, Gert, would be Christ's avenger, although everyone doubted that he had ever seen the inside of a church. One day Max organised a group of his friends to jump Gert and they gave him the hiding of his life. This never stopped him, but from then on, he made sure that he was never alone.

Hendrik, the second son, was the gardener, who managed to coax all kinds of vegetables from the small patch of clay that he called a garden. He was not a clever child, slower than most mentally, but he was diligent and quiet around the house. With his dark hair and round black eyes, he was possibly the best-looking of the four boys.

The third son, Petrus, was the student, and his mother's favourite. He had the ambition she wanted all her children to have. He spent most of his time at school, either studying or playing sports. School to him was an escape from the poverty and misery that was home, because at school, he was an equal to those boys who came from wealthier families. His shoes may have been a lot more scuffed and his school uniform more faded and worn, but no one judged him by his parents. They accepted him for himself, and he knew that they liked him for himself.

Johan, the youngest boy, was another Gert, always untidy and more inclined to play than to help at home. His mother despaired of him in her quiet way and would try to discipline him, but without much success.

Then Ma died.

Years later, whenever Hettie spoke about Ma, she felt that she had died of overwork, and that to her death was the holiday she had never had, the rest she had always wanted. The few people in the town who knew her all said that she had died of swamp sickness, the name those who lived on the vlei called bronchitis. In those days before antibiotics were discovered, anyone who was undernourished and contracted swamp sickness usually developed pneumonia, with little chance of survival. Hettie believed that had Ma wanted to live, she may have pulled through, but her lack of will and her total exhaustion gave her far less than an average chance.

Hettie's memories of her were always that of a tired, lumpy, uncomplaining woman dressed in a faded blue shapeless dress. Work for her was seven days a week, without even a day for prayer. She remembered that Ma's dress was always clean and, whenever she had buried her head in her Ma's ample breasts or clutched at her legs looking for comfort, Ma had always smelled of lavender. Hettie's fondest memories had been of a woman who never said much, but who gave all the love she had to each one of her children. It was only years later, when Hettie returned to Brakenstroom and, eventually after much searching, found her mother's grave, that she discovered that her mother had given her her own name.

For the first five months after her mother's death, life went on as normal. Sissie, at fourteen years old, took over their mother's position and looked after the family. She continued to take in sewing, but her clientele was falling away because, even though she was a good seamstress, no one wanted to give a child work, especially work they felt would be above her capabilities. They gave her the odd job, feeling sorry for the pleading they saw in her eyes whenever she knocked at their doors.

Where Sissie was quiet and withdrawn before her mother's death, she became even more so now. She took her position as mother in the house very seriously. She attended school because she had to, not because she wanted to, but she was more absent than present as she struggled to raise a family thrust upon her.

Her older brother Gert, at fifteen, was not one to be relied on. He was too much like his father and spent most of his days with his friends either playing truant from school, either fishing in the swamp, or drinking and smoking dagga (marijuana). In one more year, he would be old enough to leave school, and then he would get a job with the South African Railways. He couldn't wait for that day and neither could Sissie, because then it would be one less mouth for her to feed.

Her brothers Hendrik and Johan tried to help her about the house, but she found it very difficult to control boys who became less controllable as the days passed, while Petrus avoided coming home as much as possible, preferring to stay at school, or study at the Carnegie Library. She was their sister, not their mother, and they felt that they did not have to listen to her. To escape her demands, Petrus spent more and more time at school, sleeping out whenever his friends invited him, while Hendrik in his quiet slow way ignored her, tending to his garden and supplying vegetables for the house whenever he could.

Corrie was too young to help. She needed a mother and Sissie took over this surrogate role to the best of her ability. Hettie, being a little older, would try to complete any chores that Sissie would pass on to her, but at nine, she was also still a child, and quickly dissolved into tears whenever Sissie reprimanded her for a job not completed.

When Hettie and Corrie played, they played with dolls that were made out of the black clay that was the garden, burned in an open fire to a degree of hardness and covered with a slither of cloth as a dress. Hendrik was the sculptor, and in their eyes his work was as beautiful as any they may have bought in a shop.

The local welfare agency visited the house often enough, reporting that the family was not wanting. They managed to find a position for Gert senior with the South African Railways as a porter, threatening to send the children to the orphanage and prosecute him for child neglect if he did not keep the position. He, for the first time in his life, earned a small pittance honestly. What he didn't spend on cheap wine, he gave to Sissie for food.

The social welfare also helped where they could. They gave money, but only when it was needed, and tended to ignore the deterioration that was slowly setting in within the family. How much could a child of fourteen achieve? They discreetly looked the other way, hoping that the problem would sort itself out.

"At any rate," the social worker reported to her supervisor, "these people, who claim to be white, have a bit of black in them. They are not our responsibility. The native affairs department should look after them. How they ever managed to own a house on this side of the road, I don't know." She shook her head knowingly, as though sharing a secret.

Most nights, Gert, still more drunk than sober in spite of his new-found employment, would slip across the road to the The Location whenever he needed to satisfy his sexual urges. The girls were quite happy to see him leave the house, although they never knew where he went or what he went for.

Sissie was undernourished, painfully thin, and had not yet menstruated, although most of the girls in her class at school had. She had learned nothing about sex from her mother. The noises she had heard from her parent's bedroom at night seemed simply a continuation of her father beating her mother. She was not party to the whispers and giggles of the girls at school, as they flirted with those boys who played in the rugby or cricket teams. Her poverty isolated her from them. She was totally ignorant of her body, although she did on occasion wonder why she still had buds for breasts, when some of the girls in her class had had a full bosom since the age of twelve.

One night, about six months after Ma's death, her father, drunk as usual after coming home from work, called her into his bedroom.

"Come here," he shouted, his words slurring and almost unintelligible.

Sissie heard him shout, but did not realize that he was calling her.

"Come here," he shouted louder when she had not come to him.

Sissie had been preparing for sleep and had tucked Hettie and Corrie in to the bed they shared. She had on her night-dress and was combing her long hair, something her mother had always insisted she did before going to bed.

She walked to the door of his bedroom and looked in. He was sitting up in bed, totally nude. She had often seen her father nude, having on numerous occasions in the past helped her mother undress him and put him to bed when he was too drunk to move. When he saw her he jumped off the bed and grabbed her by the wrist, pulling her towards him. She was confused. Not knowing what he wanted, she went with him, and when he pulled her nightdress over her head and threw her down on the bed, she started to whimper softly, scared that he would hit her in his drunken state.

"Open your fucking legs," he shouted at her as he hit her across the face with the back of his hand. Her nightdress covering her face softened the blow, but it was still hard enough to cause her to cry out with pain. She opened her legs slightly, terrified that he would hit her again, not knowing what he wanted. He placed his hands under her knees, and bent her legs. She lay limp like a doll, her eyes round with fear. He tried to enter her, but she tensed, making it more difficult for him.

"Damn you, let go," he shouted at her again, punching her in the stomach. She screamed with pain and her legs opened. Then she screamed again as he entered her.

When he was spent, he rolled onto his back and started snoring. She lay still, not knowing what had happened, crying softly. When she realized that he was asleep, she crept from the room, holding her stomach where he had punched her, tears streaming down her face.

Hettie, who was still awake, had heard everything. To her, nothing out of the ordinary had happened. This is what happened to Ma, so it was normal for it to happen to Sissie who had taken her place.

She lay in bed waiting for Sissie to go to the kitchen and make a cup of tea as Ma had, so she was surprised when Sissie crept into bed next to her, still sobbing from pain and confusion.

"Don't cry, Sissie," she said, trying to comfort her. "Ma always made tea in the kitchen. Let me make you a cup." But Sissie held her tightly and buried her head in her shoulder, shuddering as each sob broke through her clenched lips.

Sissie had no one to turn to. At school the next day, her teacher noticed the dark rings under the child's eyes, but thought nothing of it. Sex education was taboo at school, frowned on by the Department of Education. The last thought that would have entered any teacher's mind was a sexual abuse problem among any of the children. A child was supposed to learn about sex from their parents, while the parents left that responsibility to the school.

Having sex with her father soon became a regular occurrence. The initial pain Sissie had felt as he entered her was no longer present. She never did enjoy the act, but he was her father, and she accepted it as a way of life. To the other children, it was the norm;

no one had ever taught them otherwise. Their father never beat Sissie like he did their mother, possibly because she quickly complied to his demands. For Sissie, sex with him became as natural as brushing her teeth before bed. He never made love to her. If he had, she may have realised that what was happening was unnatural. It was simply an act of pure lust at its most basic. The only gripe she did have was that he often woke her, interrupting her sleep.

Seven months later he started making sexual demands on Hettie and Corrie. Sissie did not protest. In a way she was relieved, because it took some pressure off her. She had also discovered that she could coax more money out of him if she met his cravings, money he usually spent on drink, and money that she needed to run the house.

The boys at first thought it strange that she should spend time in her father's bedroom, and although Gert, the eldest son, knew a little about sex, as almost every boy does on reaching puberty, he did not regard it as unnatural for his father to lie with his sister. He had only just turned fifteen, and was still exploring his own body and that of any willing girl, including his younger sisters.

The other boys knew hardly anything about sex. Hendrik was too involved in his gardening to notice anything unusual, and Petrus, at twelve, did not think much of it. His studies consumed most of his attention. Johan was simply too young to know that events at home were anything but ordinary.

With time, the girls became so accustomed to having sex with their father that they thought nothing of offering themselves to any of their brother's friends for a reward. It made them popular with the boys and gave them the attention they should have received from a loving parent. When, after a while, they found that they could demand a sum of money, rather than an ice cream or a sweet, they became even more active.

"Hettie, come into the bushes with me and I will give you a sucker," they would laugh at her. She did not understand the joke and would refuse, knowing that a tickey (three pence), or even a sixpence if she let them touch her rather than simply look at her, would please Sissie even more.

"I will push you for a sixpence," she would argue. She used the word push and not fuck, as the boys did, because fuck was a swear word, and Ma had always said that she must never swear.

Often, though, the boys would grab Corrie, pull down her panties, and simply look and touch without paying. This would make Hettie mad, as she felt she was being cheated out of money. She would then call to Sissie, who usually came running, swinging a broom.

"Leave her alone," Sissie would shout. "If you want to look, you must pay," and she would chase them all from the yard, catching the odd head with the broom as she ran.

Without realizing that anything was wrong, Sissie had created the youngest and cheapest brothel in the town. To Hettie and Corrie, it was a game that gave them pocket money, something their father never gave them.

This went on for about a year. By now Hettie was almost eleven years old and Corrie nine. Sissie at sixteen was beginning to look as tired as her mother had looked. She had begun to suspect that what she and her sisters were doing was wrong. Books she read at school described the sexual act as an act of love and the culmination of love between two people. She began to look on her father as a monster and slowly began to reject him, pretending not to hear when he called her to the bedroom at night.

Then one day at school, she started menstruating. She was sitting in class when she felt something trickle down her leg. She looked down in horror to see a thin river of blood oozing from under her dress. She stood up screaming, and Mrs. Uys, her teacher, immediately grasped the situation and took her to the sick bay.

"Stop crying, Sissie," Mrs. Uys said, trying to calm the hysterical child, "it is nothing to be scared of. Your body is telling you that you are now a woman."

Sissie looked at the blood, still not knowing where it was coming from.

"But, where is the blood coming from?" she sobbed.

Mrs. Uys looked at her, surprised. Usually at this age most of the girls she had helped knew about menstruation. Whenever she helped a girl in the clinic, it was because the child had started menstruating unexpectedly, usually on the playground, and was embarrassed rather than frightened.

"Do you know why you are bleeding?" she asked Sissie.

Sissie shook her head, wiping her eyes with the back of her hand, and took a Kleenex from the box held out to her, blowing her nose with care.

Mrs. Uys gave a sigh of frustration.

"If only parents realised . . ." she thought. She took a chart that she had specially prepared for occasions like this, and against all school regulations, explained to Sissie what was happening to her body.

She told Sissie about pregnancy, but she did not describe the sex act. She explained how, once a month, if the egg her ovary released was not fertilised and embedded in the wall of the womb where it would grow into a baby, her body cleansed the womb, preparing it for the next fertilisation cycle.

"But . . . but . . . how does the egg get fertilized?" Sissie asked hesitantly.

Mrs. Uys evaded the question. "That is something you must ask your mother," she answered. Then, remembering that Sissie did not have a mother, she explained the sex act to her. For the first time Sissie knew that what was happening to her and her sisters at home was terribly wrong.

Hettie and Corrie had become so accustomed to casual intercourse, that they would often accost a stranger in the street, saying to him in Afrikaans, *"Meneer, as jy my 'n sjilling gee, sal ek jou stoot,"* which meant, "Sir, if you give me a shilling, I will push you." They had increased their price to a shilling because Hettie had worked out that if a boy could pay a sixpence, an adult could pay a shilling.

Most of the men they accosted would look at these two children with their unkempt hair, dirty faces and bare feet, and not understand what they wanted. Some would give them a shilling, and then try to shake them off, as the girls grabbed their hand and tried to pull them into the bushes at the side of the road. They could not understand why they kept shouting, *"Kom, ek sal jou stoot . . .* come, I will push you."

As time passed, Sissie became more and more worried. She spoke to the girls and tried to stop them, but they laughed and refused to listen to her. The shilling, when they received one, meant a great deal to them.

"You must stop," Sissie would shout at them. "If you don't, you will have a baby, and then there will be trouble."

"Don't talk rubbish," Hettie would snap, not understanding her, and she would run off with Corrie, laughing at her sister's crazy ideas, while Sissie stood in frustration, not knowing how to discipline her.

Sissie still allowed her father to abuse her, but was far less accommodating than in the past. She had learned to constrict her vaginal muscles, making it more difficult for him to enter her, but not realizing that at the same time it gave him more pleasure. She gradually increased her resistance by simply making sure she was not around when he called for her. She found work as a waitress at one of the many cafes in town, staying out late at night. She hoped that he would be asleep by the time she returned to the house, but Gert simply used one of the younger girls to satisfy his unnatural lust, making her feel guilty.

"Stop it," she screamed at him one night after she found Corrie in his bed. "Leave her alone."

"Go fuck yourself," he mumbled at her in his drunken stupor, angry at being woken up.

"If you don't stop with Corrie then I will tell the social worker," she threatened.

"Go tell her," he shouted. "Tell that stupid bitch to come. I will show her what she needs, she and her fancy ways. That's her problem. She hasn't had it for a long time." He reached out to grab her, but Sissie avoided him and, taking Corrie by the wrist, pulled her from the room.

Petrus found her in the kitchen crying.

"What is wrong, Sissie?" he asked, concerned. Of all the boys he was the only one disturbed by the events at home. He was beginning to understand sex and had started to realize that girls simply do not give themselves to everyone.

"It is enough," she said through her tears. "This has got to stop."

"Jannie says Hettie and Corrie are whores," Petrus said hesitantly.

She looked up and banged the table with her hand.

"They are not," she shouted. "They are babies, they just don't understand."

"But then, what about you and him. You know that you must also stop."

She started crying. "How can I? If I don't then he will take Hettie or Corrie. How can I stop him?"

"We will find a way," Petrus whispered determinedly. "We must find a way."

He tried to speak to Gert and Johan, but they weren't interested. He tried to approach his teachers at school, but didn't know how to broach the subject. He was worried and this continual worry started to affect his schoolwork.

And then Sissie fell pregnant.

She was not sure what was happening to her. She stopped menstruating after having been quite regular for at least five months. This she took as a blessing rather than a problem. She noticed that her breasts were developing and her clothes less loose around her waist, but she assumed that it was part of growing up.

"I am becoming more like the other girls," she would say to herself and would pose in front of a mirror, pleased at her developing cleavage, making her more like them.

At home she wore the same shapeless dresses her mother had worn, but at school she had to wear the standard regulation school uniform, and the girdle (belt) around her waist became tighter and tighter. She started to eat less, thinking that she was becoming fat, but as her belly swelled more and more, she became confused.

It was only after she was seven months pregnant that her father discovered her condition. Intercourse had become painful for her and she cried out whenever he tried to penetrate her. In his drunken state, he was not aware of her distress. Then one night, after she returned home late from work, he surprised her while she was undressing and immediately recognized her condition when he saw her swollen belly.

"Wat die Duiwel! What the devil," he shouted, alarmed at what he saw. "You are pregnant!" He lashed out at her with the back of his hand, catching her across the mouth. She collapsed in a heap, crying and shocked, not understanding what he was shouting.

"I am not," she cried, "I am not." She looked up at him, her eyes wide with terror, her hand against the side of her face where he had hit her, blood oozing from the corner of her mouth.

"I am not . . ." she whispered to herself, as it dawned on her that she was indeed pregnant. He looked at her where she lay, and then angrily kicked her in her side, swearing at her as he did so. Hettie and Corrie huddled in a corner of the room, their eyes round with fear. He kicked her again and Sissie cried out with pain. Hettie threw herself at his legs and held onto them to stop him from kicking Sissie for a third time. He punched at her, but caught the top of her head.

"Los haar, leave her," she sobbed. "I hate you! I hate you!"

He looked at her as she tried again to hold his legs, then he looked at Sissie. He blamed her for falling pregnant, for not taking the necessary precautions, not realizing that no one had ever told her that precautions were necessary. The three boys, who had woken with the screams, stood at the door to the room, not knowing what was happening. Petrus, thinking that his father was giving Hettie a beating, ran to Gert and started pulling him away from her.

"Please, Pa," he pleaded, "she is a baby. Leave her."

Gert looked at the two girls lying on the floor in front of him. Hettie had crawled to Sissie and was kissing her, trying to console her as best she could. His anger had cleared. He shook Petrus off him, turned and walked to his room, slamming the door behind him. He sat on his bed, his head in his trembling hands. He was both angry and scared, realizing that her pregnancy was illegal, that she was under age and that he was the father.

In the children's room, Petrus joined Hettie in trying to console Sissie.

"Don't cry, Sissie," Hettie was whispering softly. "Come, I will make you a cup of tea." She tried to pull her sister gently towards the kitchen, but Sissie couldn't move. Petrus looked at his two sisters in front of him. Blood was slowly staining Sissie's night-dress as she lay on the floor. He looked at his father's closed bedroom door not knowing what to do. He heard him muttering and opened the door slowly, carefully looking inside the room.

"What now?" he heard his father say to himself. "What the fuck am I going to do now? If that social worker finds out about Sissie, then I am in one fucking mess."

Scared at what he heard, Petrus ran from the house confused, but knowing that Sissie needed help.

After a few minutes, Gert walked back into the girls' bedroom. He saw that Sissie was bleeding heavily.

"Hettie," he shouted, "put some clothes on her." He pointed to Sissie. "She is coming with me."

Hettie stood up, cautiously avoiding him. Then for the first time she saw the blood.

"There's blood. Sissie is going to die," she screamed. "There is blood." She pointed to the widening red puddle on the floor where Sissie lay.

Gert walked closer to them and Sissie, scared that he was going to kick her again, tried to move, but cried out with pain, clutching her stomach. Gert, scared now that she was dying, lifted her in his arms. He carried her from the house across the road to the house of the prostitutes he had visited so often.

Their house was small, built of mud bricks with brown mud plaster roughly smoothed into semi-circular patterns. It was not painted, although the frames of the door and two windows may have been white sometime in the past. The house did not have electricity, and he could see the light of candles flickering in the windows. The stone paving leading to the front door was uneven, and he nearly fell.

"She is pregnant," he told them after they had opened the door to his incessant banging. "Fix her up. I will pay you."

Two black girls looked at this white man in front of them, their eyes wide with horror at what they saw. They wore grey night-dresses that silhouetted their bodies against the candle light of the room behind them.

"Fuck off, you," they shouted at Gert. "Voetsak jou vuil ding! Bugger off, you filthy thing, we are busy."

"Help her. I will pay you," he repeated. He put Sissie on the ground at their feet. She groaned with pain.

They knelt next to Sissie as she lay at the door.

"Liewe Hemel, Dear God, what have you done to her," one of them whispered, her hand covering her mouth in shock. "You pig!" she shouted. "You filthy pig!" and she started hitting him with her fists. He turned and stumbled into the darkness. She spat after him and turned back to Sissie.

"Fix her!" he shouted back at them. "Fix her, damn you. I will pay." He ran off into the darkness.

They comforted the sobbing girl lying at their feet, shock in their faces. Sissie's nightdress was soaked in blood. They carried her carefully into the house and lay her down on one of their beds.

"What did he do to you?" they asked her, but Sissie sobbed silently, not saying anything. She was terrified by the candle-lit room and by the women with their white eyes in their black shiny faces that reflected the orange light from the candles. They explored her body. The pain that had moved to her crotch sharpened, and she bit her lip, grunting as it peaked. They stripped her, cutting away her blood-stained nightdress with a sharp knife and, as they washed the blood from her, they saw the bruise where she had been kicked.

"That filthy white pig," one of them said, "he deserves to die."

To them, a girl became a woman at twelve, so they were not surprised at Sissie's pregnancy, but they were horrified at what had been done to her and suspected that she was aborting. They examined her and found that her cervix was far too dilated for her to be taken home. They knew that if they did call in the authorities, they would be accused of causing the abortion.

They gave her a brown pill that they had made from various herbs they had collected in the veldt, and poured a glass full of an infusion from a bottle they kept in a cupboard. Squeezing her cheeks to force her mouth open, they poured the bitter liquid down her throat. Sissie coughed and tried to spit it out, but they kept her mouth closed. Her trembling gradually stopped and she lay peacefully, as though sleeping. After a while she started hallucinating calling out to her mother. "Ma, ach Ma, help me, please Ma, help me."

One of the women held her hand and wiped her brow and whispered to her softly, "I am here, my child, don't be afraid. I will help you."

Sissie relaxed, squeezing the hand that held hers with every contraction, pushing when she was told to push. The sweat poured from her face.

Her contractions came closer together, but she was too drugged to be aware of anything. When she was fully dilated, one of the woman pressed down gently on her stomach while the other slipped her hands into the vaginal cavity, stretching the walls while she coaxed the head of the baby into the world.

They were shocked when they saw the baby. Because Sissie was so small and had kept her weight down by not eating, they had thought she was three to four months pregnant. When they saw that the baby was alive although very small, they knew then that she had been closer to seven months. They also knew that the baby did not have much chance of survival, even with medical assistance, and they cursed this white man who had brought this girl to them.

"We must take her home and the ambulance must come and take her to hospital," one said to the other.

They called one of the men who had been patiently waiting outside the house in the backyard. He gently lifted Sissie wrapped warmly in a blanket with the baby in her arms and carried her carefully across the mud road. Sissie was still drugged from the drink they had given her. She was haemorrhaging, but less than before, and the blood was dark, not the bright red of arterial blood.

In the meantime Petrus had run to the home of one of his school friends. They phoned the police and the hospital, asking for an ambulance. By the time the ambulance driver had found the house in Vlei Street, Sissie was back in her bed, with the baby in her arms, delirious and semiconscious. Gert was nowhere to be found.

When the hospital doctor on duty saw Sissie's bruises, he was shocked. He immediately put her on a drip to replace the blood she had lost and gave her a sedative. Realizing that the baby was premature, he shook his head sadly. There was very little he could do.

When Sergeant Marais went to arrest Gert, he took the social worker with him. They found Gert lying in the sun in the yard, drunk as usual.

"*Meneer*, Mister," Sergeant Marais said to him, "are you Gert van Tonder?"

Gert did not answer. He repeated the question. Gert opened one eye and looked at the policeman that stood in front of him.

"Ach, yes," he mumbled and closed his eyes.

"Well sir," Sergeant Marais asked, "will you come with me, please. We have a few questions to ask you at the station."

Gert thought of resisting, but this huge man dressed in khaki standing above him looked even bigger from where he lay. He realised that resistance would be futile. He tried to stand, but couldn't. Sergeant Marais lifted him and carried him to the police van under one arm, while the children looked on in amazement.

"I will see that you go to jail for this, Gert van Tonder," the social worker shouted after them as Sergeant Marais, carrying Gert, walked past her.

Gert raised his head and focussed one eye on her.

"Fuck you!" he shouted at her. "That's just what you need, you tight-arsed stupid bitch. You need a good fuck!"

She turned bright red, embarrassed by his words. She shooed the children into her car and drove off, the gears of the car clashing in anger.

Gert was convicted and imprisoned for five years for molesting the three girls. Sissie refused to talk about the events at home, but Hettie and Corrie were like two little chatterboxes and told the public prosecutor everything at the trial.

When the magistrate, trying to understand the full implications of the events at their house, asked Hettie after she had told her story, ". . . and *then* what did you do?" Hettie answered, pleased at the new dress she wore and at all the attention she was receiving, "After that he gave me the shilling and I pushed him."

"You what?" the Magistrate asked.

"I pushed him," she replied, smiling at the ripple of laughter that echoed through the court.

"Quiet! Quiet!" the magistrate shouted banging his gavel loudly, still perplexed at her answer. When the court quietened down, he turned to the public prosecutor.

"What does she mean when she says she 'pushed' him?" he asked. The prosecutor, horrified, looked around the room for help. Everyone tittered.

"Well?" the magistrate asked again, expecting an immediate reply.

"Err . . ." the prosecutor began, "it . . .uhh . . . means . . . sir . . . that uhh . . . she had oral sex with him, uhh . . . sir," he said, turning crimson.

And then, quite innocently, and with the most angelic of expressions on her face, Hettie turned to the horrified magistrate, and in her most polite voice asked, "Would Uncle like me to push him also? It will only cost Uncle a shilling."

Everyone in the courtroom exploded in laughter. The public prosecutor bent his head under his desk and tried to hide his embarrassment while Gert's lawyer was forced to turn his back so that his client could not see his uncontrolled laughter. Gert sat in the dock, oblivious to all around him. It took the magistrate almost five minutes of constant banging his gavel to bring the court under control once again.

He looked at Hettie as she sat in the witness box. She was looking around the courtroom, puzzled now at the laughter. She knew that she was the cause of it, but was not sure why.

"Thank you, you can take her away," the magistrate said brusquely to the public prosecutor.

Hettie was led from the witness stand. As she walked to her seat next to Corrie, any titter that followed her brought a quick bang from the gavel.

"Next witness," the magistrate called to the public prosecutor who was by now a bundle of nerves.

"I call on Corr . . . Corr . . . . Petrus van Tonder," he said, suddenly changing his mind. A ripple of laughter rang through the court once more.

The magistrate banged his gavel loudly, glared at the public prosecutor under his thick bushy eyebrows and declared, "This court is adjourned. Mr. Pieterse," he shouted at the public prosecutor, "when we resume, you will see to it that your witnesses present their evidence in a proper manner."

"Yes, sir," the public prosecutor said, shrinking into himself with embarrassment, knowing that his career had taken a number of steps in the wrong direction.

"And," the magistrate continued, glaring at the court, "it will be without an audience."

With his black gown flaring behind him, he stormed from the court. As he passed Hettie, he looked down at her, piqued. She smiled up at him, blissfully unaware of the confusion she had created.

Hettie never saw any of her family again. The boys were placed in an orphanage, and the girls were all found families in various towns throughout South Africa. Her adopted family did not encourage her to keep in touch with her brothers and sisters, and attempts by them to contact her were quietly discouraged. Her memories faded with time, and her new family, to protect her, told her very little about her childhood. When she asked questions about her adoption, which they did not hide from her, they told her about her family and about her brothers and sisters, but they did not tell her that she had been abused as a child. Happiness and love made her forget, not that her memories were unpleasant, but they were events that could easily be forgotten, especially for a child.

Gert was sentenced to five years imprisonment for child rape and molestation, but effectively served only three years. When he was released from jail, he did not try to bring his family together, but instead moved to a small town in the Cape where he married a widow with children.

When she was nineteen years old, Hettie received a letter from Petrus. She was a student nurse at the Johannesburg General hospital, renting a flat close by and only going home the occasional weekend. Petrus' letter, addressed to her at the flat, was a surprise.

She replied with great hesitation and after a great deal of introspection. She was nervous. What she remembered of her past was not pleasant, so she suppressed the memories as much as she could, trying not to think about what to her now seemed like a very bad dream. When Petrus received her letter, he phoned her. She found it strange to talk to someone who said he was her brother, but eventually after a great deal of persuasion, she agreed to his suggestion that they should meet in Brakenstroom. He gave her an address and on the arranged weekend, telling her parents she was staying with a friend, she caught the Greyhound bus to Brakenstroom.

She remembered nothing of the town, and when she walked down Vlei Street, which was now tarred and bordered with graceful willows on the river side of the sidewalk, there was nothing to remind her of her youth. The townhouse developments she walked past were all new. She enjoyed the warmth of the summer morning, smiling as she heard the laughter of children playing in the gardens.

A young man approached her.

"Hello." He extended his hand. "You must be Hettie. I am your brother Petrus."

She held out her hand, and hesitated. It was as though she was looking at a male version of herself, with the same sunburned blond hair and blue eyes framed by white eyebrows. He had a pleasant open face tanned golden by the sun, with a faint sprinkling of freckles across his nose, and his smile stretched from ear to ear, framing teeth that were beautiful in their white uniformity.

A thought entered her head, "What if I were not Hettie," and she smiled to herself. "I don't think I would be upset at being approached by him."

She took his outstretched hand in hers. "Yes, I am Hettie," she answered, "although most of my friends call me Hester." She winced as he gripped her hand a bit too hard, then she had to bite back a scream as he pulled her to him and hugged her.

"My God," he said, "I am so pleased to see you. You are . . . really, very beautiful."

She pushed him away from her, but he held her by the shoulders and studied her face carefully. Her long blonde hair was fashionably cut, and hung loosely down her back. Her eyes were framed by a hint of blue mascara and she wore a light pink pearl lipstick that accented her full mouth. She was neatly dressed in a white dress with a thick red belt that made her waistline look thinner than it actually was. Weekends at home lying at the pool had given her a golden tan, but she had protected her face from the sun, and her skin was free of freckles.

"Life has been kind to you," he said, admiring her. "You must have wonderful parents."

"Yes," she said hesitantly, "I do, but what about you?"

"I was lucky," he answered. "I won a scholarship at the orphanage and am studying Medicine at Pretoria. Otherwise growing up in an orphanage is not that much fun."

His remark made her feel guilty. "I . . . I am sorry," she said.

He felt awkward with her discomfort, and turned and pointed at the house they were standing in front of. "This is the house we grew up in," he said, pointing to a neatly cut hawthorn hedge hiding the house. The garden gate was painted silver and a red concrete path lined with standard roses led to a wide red veranda that ran the width of the house. He opened the gate and turned to her, holding out his hand. "Come, Sissie and Hendrik have invited us to tea."

"Sissie?" she asked, frowning, as some scraps of memory drifted back, "Sissie . . . she is my real mother? I remember a woman that smelled of . . . I can't remember."

He was puzzled. "No," he answered slowly, "Sissie is our sister and Hendrik is our brother." He hesitated. "Let us sit over there for a minute," he pointed to a bench under a willow tree on the opposite side of the road. "There is much you seem to have forgotten."

They walked across the road and sat down on the bench. After standing in the hot sun, the cool shade of the willow was welcome.

"Did your parents tell you anything about us?" he asked.

"Yes," she answered, "but not very much. They simply told me that I was adopted and had a family, but I have forgotten a great deal of what they told me, especially names. When I received your letter, well . . . I think I came more out of curiosity than anything else."

He frowned at her words.

"I will try and fill you in with as much as I can, but quickly, because Sissie and Hendrik are both looking forward to meeting us and I don't think we should keep them waiting. Sissie is our eldest sister, and she went to live with a family in Wolmaranstad," he began, taking both her hands in his. They were trembling slightly and he held them tightly. "As soon as Sissie turned twenty-one, she came back to Brakenstroom and moved into our old house. The house had been in our mother's name, and in her will she had left it to all of us when she died. Sissie makes a living by sewing. She is not rich, but she survives. Hendrik lives with her. He works for the municipality as a gardener. We have an older brother, Gert. He joined the South African Railways and lives in Kimberly. Our younger brother, Johan was killed on the Angolan border while doing his military service, and Corrie, our youngest sister, lives in Canada. I have tried to contact her, but my letters are returned address unknown."

"Who is our father?" she asked hesitantly.

"He died three years ago," Petrus answered. "He lived somewhere in the Cape. That is about all I know."

"And . . . and our mother?"

"I can't tell you much about her," Petrus answered. "I was too young when she died. Memories of her are a blur. You can ask Sissie, she may know more about her." He stood up. "But come," he said, holding out a hand to her, "I think we should be going. They're waiting for us."

Hettie stood up and brushed her white skirt across her legs. Petrus took her arm and they walked slowly across the road.

They sat in the living room drinking tea and eating a cake that Sissie had baked. Hettie found it strange that Sissie and Hendrik were her brother and sister, because they were all so different from each other. Where she and Petrus were blonde and light-skinned, they were dark, with black hair and an olive complexion.

"Do you know where the others are?" Petrus asked politely.

"Corrie is living in Canada," Sissie began.

Hettie listened, but heard very little. The room they were sitting in felt familiar, yet it was strange. She sat restlessly, not listening to Sissie while she talked. After a while she stood up and walked to where she knew a bedroom ought to be. She looked in through the open door. It was neat and tidy, with a table next to the bed in front of the window. A pipe lay in an ashtray on the table. The room felt familiar, but the bed was too small; somehow it did not look right. From the corner of her eye she saw a shadow move, and turned her head. Then she heard the 'klink' of a cup to a saucer. The years seemed to fall away as her suppressed memories came flooding back. She walked to where she knew the kitchen was. She opened the door and smelled a faint hint of lavender.

"Ma . . ." she called hesitantly, "Ma, where are you . . ." and she started crying.

Jan and Toby

1

LIKE MOST TOWNS throughout the world, Brakenstroom had its very wealthy families and its not so wealthy families. This wealth had been accumulated through good business practice and hard work, but in Brakenstroom, a large number of the super rich had made their fortune by dealing in illicit diamonds. IDB, short for illicit diamond buying, was a national pastime for those prepared to take the risk. One could make as much money as the drug barons of today, but it was clean money in that it did not hurt a third party the way drugs do. It was only the diamond mining companies that were hurt and all they lost was a small percentage of their profits. When a dealer was caught, he usually paid a large fine, or would spend a few years in jail and on being released would return red-faced to a society that laughed at him. His only crime in their eyes was that he had been caught.

Jan Ellis had always wanted to be a policeman, and after he had matriculated, he joined the South African Police Force (SAP). He was an idealist and loved his work, rising rapidly through the ranks as he gained the trust and respect of his superiors.

When he turned twenty-five, he married his childhood sweetheart, Sannie Pretorius, and over the next six years fathered three children, a son and two daughters. He considered himself to be a lucky man with a wonderful family. As a member of the Nederduitse Gereformeerde Kerk, he was a staunch Calvanist, serving as an Ouderling (elder) for many years.

At the outbreak of the Second World War, his sympathies had lain with the Germans. This viewpoint was held by many Afrikaaners, not so much in that they were pro-Nazi, but they were anti--British, a carry-over from the Anglo-Boer War, where almost all Afrikaner families had lost a loved one to the infamous British concentration camps. Jan's sympathies, although a close secret, gradually became known to his superiors, and in the English Government of General Jan Christian Smuts, this was the only blot on an otherwise very distinguished service record. Unfortunately for him, promotion was frozen and he became disillusioned in his work.

In 1948 the National Party came to power and the blot on his record was removed. He was fifty-four years old and after six years, planned to take early retirement, but when he calculated the amount of pension he would be receiving, he felt bitter and blamed the Smuts Government for cheating him out of a promotion that should have been his. His dislike of anything and everything that was English became even more profound.

"These Rooinekke think they conquered us in the Boer War, but we will end up the conquerors. We control the country. Stay away from them."

Geert, Jan's son, always remembered his father's words, and although in his years at University he became less rigid in his thinking, he nevertheless regarded the English-speaking South African as a curiosity to be tolerated and avoided. During his years of study he did develop a degree of respect for the few English-speaking students in his class, and actually looked forward to any debate they were involved in, but he kept his distance, and his immediate social group were all Afrikaners.

Jan felt proud when Geert qualified as an attorney and found a position with a law firm in Brakenstroom. His daughters, Karina and Esther, married and moved to towns elsewhere in South Africa.

Life for Jan, with the exception of his pension, was exactly as he and Sannie had planned it should be. They had a beautiful home, and wonderful children and grandchildren, all of them God-fearing and regular churchgoers. They were solid Afrikaners, and all were card-holding members of the National Party.

They made a point of visiting Brakenstroom at least once a month. They loved the quiet countryside of the highveld and especially the town, with its graceful willow trees bordering the quiet walks along the banks of the Brak River. The ride from Johannesburg where Jan was stationed was only two hours by car, and he was inclined to speed along the tarred narrow road to what he felt was a well-earned rest from the hustle and bustle of the city. The two girls, his daughters and their families, lived a great deal further from Johannesburg, so he and Sannie visited Geert almost every second or third weekend, with the girls and their families often meeting them there when they all camped at the Brakenstroom dam. Sannie loved the town so much that she wanted Jan to buy a property for their retirement, but Jan dreamed of retiring in Hermanus.

"What would you do in Hermanus?" she would ask him, knowing full well that whenever they went to the sea, Jan spent most of his days fishing. "All you would do is fish. You can't do that every day for the rest of your life. Better we buy in Brakenstroom, where we will be close to the children . . . and grandchildren," she would sometimes add, knowing that this was his weak spot.

Jan would grunt and ignore her, concentrating on his driving. She would continue. "Well, perhaps we can talk the children into buying a cottage at Struisbaai with us. They could spend most of the summer there."

Struisbaai was a beach on the garden route between Plettenberg Bay and Hermanus. It had only just been opened up to the public and property was selling extremely well. Many Afrikaner families were buying land there with the intention of building comfortable holiday cottages. "Buy early" was the thought, because land on the garden route was at a premium, and prices would soon escalate.

". . . also the fishing is good," Jan would say, as he leafed through brochures Sannie put before him, but he hesitated to pick up the phone and contact the agents because he did not have enough money.

Geert started earning a reasonable salary and was enjoying spending it. He was a hard and conscientious worker, very quickly building up a strong client base. His promptness with an assignment earned him the respect of his employers and it was not long before he was invited to join the firm as a junior partner. On the social side, without being aware of it, he became the most sought after bachelor in town, but he had no intention of settling down. Girls were to be enjoyed, not married and there were plenty around, but he soon tired of the continual social whirl. He didn't enjoy his work as much as he thought he would, and he believed that there must be something better.

"Dad," he said to his father one day as they sat in the garden drinking beer, "I would like to study further. I want to sit for an advocate."

"As I understand it," Jan said after a few minutes thought, "this means that you will not be earning for some time."

"Yes, Dad," Geert answered.

"Then how will you live?"

"Uh," Geert mumbled, "I have a little bit saved, but I was hoping you would help me with a loan."

Jan did not answer immediately, but looked at his beer, watching the droplets on the outside of the glass coalesce as they rivered their way to the table. Then he said carefully, "You know, of course, that a policeman does not earn very much."

"Yes Dad," Geert said, feeling terrible that he had brought up the subject, "but I will pay you back and with interest after I have qualified."

"That's not the point," Jan said. "I am not earning a big wage and your mother and I still have to pay back your study loan. Can you wait a few years?"

"Yes Dad," Geert answered, trying to hide his disappointment, "it can wait. I have a good job offer, and who knows, in a few years' time I could possibly save enough myself." On an impulse he leaned forward and kissed Jan on the cheek. "Dad," he whispered, "I know that you would help me if you could."

Jan hugged him. "You are a good son," he said, his voice thick with emotion. "You are a son any man would be proud to have. We will try and work out a plan."

Geert met Jenny at a friend's wedding. In later years, he often wondered whether the bride had not contrived the meeting as an act of revenge, because at one stage he had been intimate with her. She had expected a commitment from him which he was not ready to give, and she did not want to wait. His seat at the wedding reception was next to Jenny Carruthers. She was alone because her boyfriend, Chris, was playing provincial cricket. He had often seen Jenny at the country club or the occasional party, always surrounded by men attracted to her blonde beauty like moths to a flame, but because she was English, she was completely alien to him. She was seriously involved with Chris, one of the English-speaking students who had studied law with Geert. Chris was a fine athlete and captained the Brakenstroom cricket team. It had become for her simply a matter of, "When he has completed his articles, Chris and I will announce our engagement." Jenny knew it, the town knew it, and their parents expected it.

When Geert realized that he would be sitting next to Jenny, he looked around the hall for another empty seat and silently swore under his breath when he saw that there were none.

"This is Suzanne's doing," he thought. "She knows that I am not fond of the English."

He looked at the other couples that sat at his table. They were all people he had seen at some stage or other in the town, and they were all English.

"Well," he thought as he pulled out his chair to sit down, "this wedding won't see me for long."

Jenny sat with her back half turned towards him. She was in earnest conversation with the woman on her right and didn't noticed him as he sat down. She leaned back in her chair as he sat down, and he bumped her, causing her to spill some of the red wine she was sipping down the front of her dress.

"Ach, I am so sorry," he said in English, his Afrikaans accent thicker than usual with his embarrassment. She put the glass of wine on the table and grabbed for a napkin.

"It's okay," she replied angrily, dabbing at the small red stain on her dress. "Hopefully it will wash out." She frowned at him, and he felt his face reddening.

"My mother always said that one must put salt on a wine stain before it dries," he said, and taking the salt cellar from the table, he sprinkled her dress liberally. Her dress was cut low, and most of the salt fell down her cleavage.

"Stop that, you idiot," she said angrily pushing him away. "What do you think you are doing?"

"I am so sorry. Please forgive me." He reached out a hand as though to dust the salt from her breast, then thought better of it and pulled his hand back. She had watched his hand approaching her, and raised her arm defensively. He retreated, stumbled against the table, reached a hand behind him to steady himself and sent the glass of wine flying.

"Man, that was so stupid of me," he said to himself in Afrikaans. He felt clumsy and awkward, something that was foreign to him, because he was always in control. He turned to the guests at the table who had all scattered as the wine flew in their direction. "I am so sorry, I am so sorry," he apologized, trying to mop up the wine with a table napkin then, turning to Jenny, he mumbled in Afrikaans, "Shit, man, but I am behaving like a bloody idiot." Then he said to her in English, his accent becoming even more pronounced by his nervousness, "Please, that was an accident. I hope I haven't spoiled your dress."

She had watched his antics and had nearly laughed at his embarrassment, but she caught herself and said, watching his hands carefully, "It can't be helped, it was an accident, hopefully it won't stain."

"Well, if you will let me take it to a dry cleaner's, I will pay all costs," he offered gallantly.

"That won't be necessary," she said and turned her back on him.

Once again he felt the blood rush to his face, hurt by her snub. He looked at the other guests at the table. They had all resumed their seats and were looking at him apprehensively. He gave a sickly smile and sat down, his face a mask of despair.

As the bride and groom entered the reception hall, everyone stood up and applauded. Jenny, in an act of forgiveness, turned to Geert. "Don't they make a beautiful couple," she said as she joined in the applause. Her anger was gone and she gave him one of her dazzling smiles.

He was smitten. "My God, but she is beautiful," he thought and stood with his mouth open as though in a trance, his mind a blank.

"Ach, yes . . ." he started, but she turned her back to him as she watched the bridal couple walk to the main table, applauding them all the way. He looked at her blonde hair sparkling in the sunlight as it streamed through the window of the hall. A waft of her perfume floated slowly towards him and he felt heady with it.

"What is happening to me," he thought, "I am behaving like a bloody idiot."

The bridal couple reached the main table and sat down to the applause of the guests. Jenny pulled her chair towards her and started to sit down. She looked at his glass of wine on the table, then she looked at Geert and reached a hand to steady the glass as she sat. His hand reached for the table to steady himself as he sat, and for a minute it touched hers. It was a though an electric shock passed through him. She quickly withdrew her hand.

"My name is Geert Ellis," he said, noticing her act of caution, "and I promise you, I will not bump you again." He held out his hand cautiously. "You are Jenny Carruthers, I have seen you often in town. I am very sorry about your dress. If the stain does not come out I will buy you a new one." He spoke slowly, as though translating each word from Afrikaans.

"You don't have to do that," she smiled, taking his outstretched hand. "It's an old dress."

"It is a very beautiful dress," he said, "and I would think that it would cost a lot of money to buy you a new one."

"It depends who is paying. If it is my dad, then there is no problem. If it is me, then you will have to buy me a new dress," she smiled teasingly, "as long as you come with me to the dress shop and help choose it." She cocked her head to one side and her eyes laughed at him. "But I won't hold you to that."

"But I would very much like to do that," he found himself saying, nodding his head.

She looked at him and for the first time stopped smiling. She realized that he was still holding her hand and she slowly pulled her fingers from his. She searched his face for some sign of amusement, but she saw that he was quite serious. Her eyes dropped.

"Oh, you would, would you," she replied softly, and for the first time she looked flustered.

He was pleased. He had regained his composure and it was she who was now on the defensive. He was about to say something else to her, when the master of ceremonies started with the speeches.

She sneaked a glance at Geert out of the corner of her eye and smiled as though she liked what she saw. He was quite a bit taller than she was, but he was built in a stocky solid way that gave one the impression that he was much shorter than he actually was. His rugged face was tanned and his firm square jaw suggested determination, giving an aura of security. She had often seen him at various functions, but because he was Afrikaans, they never mixed socially. She had not even known his name.

As the afternoon progressed and Geert started to relax, he found that she was indeed very pleasant company and extremely easy to talk to.

"She is beautiful, and she is intelligent," he kept telling himself, "but . . . she is English."

There was no dancing, as the bride belonged to the Dutch Reformed Church, and it was not long before they were only talking to each other, oblivious of any guests around them. Time flew by as they enjoyed each others' company, and they found that they were among the last in the hall.

"Can I give you a lift home?" Geert offered.

"Thank you, but I have my own car," she replied.

"Well," and he hesitated, "can I see you again?" he asked, surprised at himself.

She looked at him and saw that he was watching her closely, to see her reaction. Their eyes locked, and it was she who eventually looked away. "I am engaged . . ." she started saying, and then changed her mind. "Yes," she said after a few moments. "Yes. I think I would like that."

He waited two days before he phoned her to ask for a date. He did not want to be seen with her in Brakenstroom. She hesitated, but when he told her that he had reserved a table at a fine restaurant in a nearby town, she accepted because she, on the other hand, did not want Chris to find out that she was dating someone else. The chances that anyone from Brakenstroom would see them were slight.

Once again they sat talking to each other oblivious of time, and when she eventually slipped into her house, it was early morning.

He phoned her every day after that, and on those evenings when she was not going out with Chris or with friends, they usually sat in his car talking. Occasionally, if her parents were out for the evening, she would invite him into the house, where they would sit in the lounge perfectly happy to be in each other's company. As soon as they heard anyone approaching the front door, he would leave by the kitchen door.

"Do you know," she said to him after they had been seeing each other for almost three weeks, "that I have seen you just about every day. I simply don't know what we have spoken about." They were in his car, her back toward the door window. He sat with his arm on the steering wheel. He couldn't take his eyes off her. She wore no makeup and her hair was uncombed, and he thought she was more beautiful than ever. He reached out to move a wisp of hair that the wind had blown across her cheek. Not sure of what he intended, she moved her hand to her face. He took it and held it in his.

"Well, I will give you a rest," he said carefully, trying to read her face as he said it, but the street light behind her cast a shadow. "I have a case in Johannesburg, and will be away for a few days."

"Oh . . . ." she said, trying not to show her disappointment. Then, taking her hand from his, she snapped, "Well that's okay, Chris and I have a few friends to visit."

The days in Johannesburg were ones of absolute misery. He found that he could not concentrate on his work. All he could think about was Jenny.

When he returned to Brakenstroom, he did not phone her. "She is a habit that I must break," he told himself, but by the third night, as he tried to work, he couldn't concentrate. His thoughts were filled with Jenny. He decided to talk to his friend Pieter, and although it was late, he dressed, drove to Pieter's house and knocked on his door.

"What the hell, don't you know what the bloody time is?" Pieter shouted as he opened the front door, then when he saw Geert, "Geert," he said warmly, "come in, come in, what is wrong?" Geert poured out all his problems over a few beers. He did not tell him Jenny's name.

"My friend," Pieter said in a quiet dignified way, "from the little you have told me, you have developed the most common diseases of all men. You are stricken with it, and there is only one cure."

All Geert heard was "disease" and "cure."

"I *am* sick," Geert mumbled. "I don't eat well, and I struggle to sleep. I find it difficult to concentrate, and I am not getting any work done. I must be coming down with something."

Pieter looked at his friend's face, at the dark circles under his eyes. "Well," he said slowly, savoring every minute of his friend's anguish, "first the cure. You will have to marry her."

Geert had his glass to his lips. As Pieter's words sank in, he went white, choked on the beer and spluttered the froth all over Pieter.

"*What!*" he shouted. "Are you mad? She is Eng . . ." and he caught himself in time before he had blurted out his secret.

"Shit, man," Pieter swore, wiping beer from his face with his handkerchief, "you are madly in love with this secret girl that you are seeing and from what you have just told me, you will never get her out of your mind. Wherever you go she will haunt you. You, my friend, are fucked and if you are fucking her, then you are even more fucked. Who is this unlucky girl?"

Geert focused his eyes slowly on Pieter, then collapsed back into the armchair, leaning his head against the headrest as Pieter's words slowly sank in. He looked up at the ceiling.

"Dear God, but I think you are right," he said quietly, almost to himself. "When I am with her, it is as though there is no time. I cannot wait for the next day so that I can see her again. I have never ever met anyone as lovely as she is, nor anyone I enjoy being with as much as I enjoy being with her. She is simply wonderful." He looked at Pieter who stood facing him, a half smile on his face as he waited to hear who it was that had snared his friend.

"Oh, shit," Geert swore as the realization of his feelings hit him. "Oh, shit. You just don't know the trouble this is going to cause." Pieter saw Geert's despair turn to elation and then back to despair, and he wondered at the girl who could do this to his friend.

"I have known you a long time," he said, "but I have never seen you like this. She must truly be exceptional. Who is she? You can trust me, I won't tell a soul."

"Uh-uh," Geert answered, shaking his head. Then, emptying his glass in one swallow, he put it on the table and wiped the froth from his mouth with the back of his hand. "Not yet. You will find out soon enough, and man, will you be surprised." He stood up, took Pieter's hand and shook it. "You are right of course, my friend. You are usually wrong with your advice, but this time you are so very right," and he walked purposefully out to his car.

"Who is it?" Pieter shouted after him. "Who is it? I will keep your secret."

Geert relented. "Jenny Carruthers" he shouted from the car.

"Stop kidding me," Pieter called back as Geert started the car. "Who is this girl you are going to marry?"

"Jenny Carruthers," Geert shouted again, putting the car into gear.

"You are mad . . . . You are fucking mad," Pieter yelled after him as the car pulled away. He watch the taillights for a few minutes, then walked into the house shaking his head.

"What were you and Geert talking about?" his wife asked him as he climbed back into bed.

"He told me that he is in love with Jenny Carruthers and that he is going to ask her to marry him," he answered, plumping the pillow.

"Ja . . ." she answered, "tell me another."

It was after midnight, but Geert drove to Jenny's house. He had to find out now, tonight, if she would marry him. The alcohol in his system gave him the Dutch courage he needed. There was a light in the kitchen, so he walked up to the front door of her house and rang the bell. The porch light came on and Elizabeth Carruthers, Jenny's mother, opened the door.

"Yes?" she asked looking at him apprehensively. "It is rater late. How can I help you?"

"Good evening Mrs. Carruthers," Geert said, the realization of what he intended to do sobering him. "Can I see Jenny?"

"Jenny?" Elizabeth asked, "It is late, she is asleep . . . perhaps if you came back tomorrow morning."

For a moment he thought that she was going to close the door, then Jenny appeared in the hallway, her eyes red, as though she had been crying. The love he felt for her welled up out of his heart, and before he was aware of it he had brushed past Elizabeth and blurted out, "Jenny, I love you and want to marry you. I have tried to stay away from you, but I can't," and he stood looking at her, anticipating her refusal.

"Oh yes, oh yes, oh yes!" she cried, throwing herself into his arms.

For a moment he stood dumbfounded, not quiet believing what he had heard. Then, as Jennie smothered him with kisses, realization set in, and he did what any young man would do in a similar set of circumstances, he let off a shout of joy that almost deafened her and brought the whole household to the door.

Jan was upset when Geert told him that he intended to marry an English girl, and his anger was vented in four-letter words throughout the day and most of the night.

Sannie, on the other hand, was delighted that Geert was getting married. The fact that her daughter-in-law would be English scared her a little, but if Geert loved her, so would she. When they met Jenny, all her fears evaporated.

"I can see why Geert lost his heart to her," she told Jan. "She is a lovely girl, and so well brought up." Jan grudgingly agreed. "Geert told me that the Carruthers want us to stay with them at their home when we go to Brakenstroom this weekend," she continued hesitatingly, waiting for his explosion.

"Is he mad!" Jan shouted. "I . . ."

"I told Geert and Jenny that we would love to," she interrupted him. "Jan, you cannot hurt Geert by refusing." He looked at her from under his thick eyebrows, then stormed from the room, swearing under his breath.

"And I want you to remember that it is your son's future bride and his parents-in-law you will be staying with," she lectured Jan in the car on their way to Brakenstroom, "and I don't care what your feelings are towards the English." She continued, "Tonight you will forget them."

Jan looked at his wife. She had on her finest dress, the one she usually wore to Nagmaal (Holy Communion). He grunted and kept his eyes fixed on the road ahead.

"You will behave, Jan," she threatened. "Remember, Geert is going to marry Jenny and nothing you do or say will stop him. He is too much like you, hard-headed, so please, no politics."

"And if he talks politics?" Jan mumbled, referring to Toby.

"Then you will politely change the subject," she answered. "You will behave correctly and keep your mouth closed."

Toby, Jenny's father, was a self-made man. He had settled in Brakenstroom as a young man when he emigrated from England. He had found work at a garage as a mechanic, and fell in love with and married Elizabeth, the owner's daughter. Determination and hard work had seen him eventually buy the garage from his father-in-law.

During the Second World War he was drafted to serve in the South African army. He left the management of his business to Elizabeth. She was able to keep it viable while he was at war and with a young daughter to look after, as well as a struggling business, life was not easy.

Toby distinguished himself in the field and soon rose to the rank of Colonel, serving with distinction in the desert and earning a medal for valor at El Alamein. With the declaration of peace, he returned to Brakenstroom with a bad limp and a left arm that was fixed at the elbow, the results of war wounds. He also returned to a business that was on the verge of bankruptcy. He was forever grateful to Elizabeth for managing their affairs in his absence and he fell in love with the daughter she had reared. Hard work and improving conditions soon pulled the business out of the red into the black, and their living standards started to improve. He was well-liked amongst the local community and was asked to stand for the town council. He won his seat and became a councillor, but although approached to expand his political career, he felt that an English-speaking South African living in a predominantly Afrikaans-speaking town like Brakenstroom had a limited political future.

When Jenny announced that she was going to marry Geert, he was surprised. Geert was an unknown, so Toby had a character search done on him and his family. He was pleased to find that Geert came from a good family, although Jan's politics did disturb him. There was the suggestion that Jan may have been a member of the Ossawa Brandwag, a right-wing terrorist group that had supported Nazi Germany during the war.

"Events will shape the course," he said to Elizabeth after she had read the report on Geert. "We will see what happens."

"Mom and Dad," Geert said in English as he ushered his parents into the Carruthers' home. "This is Toby and Elizabeth." Jan frowned when Geert spoke English.

"Good to meet you," he said in a very rusty English. Sannie and Geert breathed a sigh of relief. At least Jan was trying.

Elizabeth, seeing the effort Jan made, walked up to Sannie.

"It is so good to meet you both, " she said in fluent Afrikaans. "Our two children took us completely by surprise, but what a pleasant surprise." She turned to Jan. "I can see why my daughter fell in love with Geert," she continued. "He is already part of our family."

Toby was proud of his wife. He had forgotten that she was completely bilingual.

"Thank you," Sannie replied in Afrikaans. "None of us ever thought that Geert would marry so soon. He was always too involved in his work, but love has a strange way of working. A girl like Jenny is a treasure you seldom find."

Dinner was a braai (barbecue), with Sannie, Jenny, and Elizabeth planning the arrangements for the wedding. Toby, Jan, and Geert stood around the braai talking, and Geert breathed a sigh of relief. His father appeared to be enjoying Toby's company.

2

APPROXIMATELY A YEAR AFTER Geert and Jenny were married, Jan was promoted to Brigadier. He was offered the position as head of the South African Police force in the territory known as the Skeleton Coast, South West Africa. The promotion was due to him and the position, a relatively soft one, was for services rendered to the National Party. He was asked to take a late retirement at seventy, and he accepted, looking forward to his posting, although Sannie was unhappy that they would be so far from the children.

The Skeleton Coast and part of the Namib Desert are the most mysterious diamond fields in the world. How the diamonds ever got there is a mystery, and even more of a mystery is that they are exposed on the surface, scattered erratically in the loose stones and earth between rocky ridges. The entire area is a top security zone, controlled by the Consolidated Diamond Mining Company of South West Africa, and policed by the South African Police. It starts immediately north of the mouth of the Orange River and extends 96 kilometres wide and 352 kilometres long, running along the coast to Hottentots Bay, north of Luderitz. A second area from Hottentots Bay to south of Walvis Bay was also sealed to mining, as well as fields further up the Skeleton Coast. Jan was in charge of the entire area and was stationed at Luderitz. He and Sannie loved the dry desert air of the Namib, which was their neighbor, but as often as they could, they would fly to Johannesburg. Jan would coordinate an official visit with a visit to Brakenstroom, when Geert usually arranged for both his sisters and their families to visit at the same time.

Geert and Jenny were expecting their first child. Toby supported them while Geert studied as an advocate. This had upset Jan as he felt that it was his duty to pay for his son's education. This sense of guilt led him to make a decision that would change all their lives.

As Brigadier, he had free access to the diamond area. Every person dealing in illicit diamonds who was arrested had the diamonds confiscated and brought to Jan for safekeeping. Because diamonds were so plentiful and the area so inaccessible, the parcels were usually quite large. It did not take Jan long to realize that some of the larger stones in a parcel could easily disappear, and no one would be the wiser. To get them out of the area was just as easy. He and Sannie flew to Johannesburg at least once every month, sometimes even twice a month. It was simply a matter of carrying them out in his pocket. He was, after all, above suspicion.

He knew that if he were caught, he would be arrested and probably spend a number of years in prison. He would also receive a court martial and lose his pension. But he was bitter; after thirty-nine years in the force he felt that he had lost too much, especially under a United Party Government. Without telling Sannie, he started moving a number of the larger stones, careful to take only those that he felt would not be missed. He locked them in a safety deposit box in a bank in Johannesburg.

By the time Geert and Jenny had given him his first grandson, he had accumulated about fifty-five uncut diamonds, worth almost one million South African pounds on the open market. How he was ever going to sell them was a problem he felt would one day solve itself.

In the years since Geert and Jenny's wedding, he and Toby had developed a comfortable friendship. He grudgingly admitted that he enjoyed Toby's company, and although on the odd occasion when they did talk politics, they both avoided their prejudices. Whenever they met, he seriously considered taking Toby into his confidence. He felt that Toby, because he was in business, would know a connection or buyer for the stones. With a policeman's instincts he gradually and cautiously felt out Toby's attitude towards IDB.

Jan turned sixty-five. As a birthday present, Toby gave him a ticket to a box at Ellis Park to watch the rugby test between the Springboks and the All Blacks. The Springboks won and the two men started celebrating almost immediately. Drinks in the box had flowed freely throughout the match and flowed even faster after the win. It was winter, and by the time they arrived at Toby's house, they were both very jovial. Night had fallen and they were cold. The huge fire roaring in the fireplace in the lounge and the warm brandy that Toby had placed in his hand made Jan feel that the world was his oyster. He looked at Toby, who stood with his back to the fire.

"I really like this verdomde rooinek, (damned red-neck)" he thought. He made his decision.

"Toby," he said hesitantly in Afrikaans.

Toby looked up.

"Toby," Jan started again, "you know that I have been in the force a long time." He paused, not looking at Toby but at the amber brandy as he swilled it in his glass, catching the flames of the fire. "I have always been an exemplary policeman and have always worked hard for my convictions, but the last few years I broke a few rules."

Toby sipped at his brandy, a look of surprise on his face. He said nothing. Jan found a chair, sat in it and studied Toby's face, looking for a sign of disapproval. He saw none. He sipped at the brandy-balloon, enjoying the smell of the fumes as he drank, warmed by the fire that flowed down his gullet. "I need a partner to help me and I was hoping that you will be my partner. I will split all profits fifty-fifty."

Toby looked puzzled. "Partner in what, Jan?" he asked.

Jan took a deep breath. "Well here goes," he thought.

"My partner in selling over five million pounds in uncut diamonds," Jan said dramatically, turning his face so that Toby could not see his anxiety.

"Good God, man," Toby spluttered. "What are you talking about?"

Jan told him everything: how he had received a raw deal under the Smut's government because of his political convictions, how his pension had suffered, and how the opportunity arose to take the stones.

"But I need someone this side to sell them," he finished. "Will you help me?"

Toby realized the risk Jan had taken by confiding in him, and felt pleased that their friendship had developed to this level. He also realized what it had cost Jan to ask him to become his partner in crime and that should he agree to help him, he himself would become a criminal. Without further thought as to the consequences, or even considering the risk he was taking both for himself and his family, he answered, "Yes, Jan, I will sell them for you. I have a few connections globally who could place the stones for us. I will feel them out. "

Jan thought for a minute.

"It's okay, Jan," Toby continued misinterpreting his silence, " I appreciate the fact that you have taken me into your confidence. I like you and I like Sannie, and of course the son you have given me is a wonderful gift." He held out his hand to Jan. Jan stood up, all the fears he had carried the last few years falling from his shoulders. He took Toby's hand and shook it vigorously, then, overcome with emotion he pulled Toby towards him and hugged him.

"You are a good man," he said in Afrikaans. "You are a good friend," he repeated in English.

When Sannie and Elizabeth walked into the study, they found the two men talking excitedly to each other, but when Jan and Toby saw them, they quickly stopped. Sannie's heart nearly burst with joy; she had never ever seen her husband so happy and she was grateful to Toby for whatever he had done.

"You and Toby are such good friends," she said to Jan as they prepared for bed that night. "What are you two up to, hey?"

Jan smiled. "Yes," he said kissing her warmly, "we are good friends and we will soon be partners in a very good business."

Toby contacted an old friend that he knew from the war. The man owed him a favour, and he felt that he could trust him. His friend had recently retired and knew the illegal diamond business exceptionally well and with his help, they soon found a market in Holland and Israel for all the stones. Toby took flying lessons and bought a small light Cessna. He and Elizabeth visited Jan and Sannie regularly in South West Africa. With each visit, he took out more stones. They were both becoming very wealthy men.

At a board meeting of Diamond Fields Ltd. in 1952, the following minutes were recorded:

"Gentleman," the Chairman announced, looking at his directors as they sat in the Burmese teak-paneled boardroom, "we have a problem."

He looked up from his notes, waiting for a reaction. His directors all watched him closely. He had their attention.

"The photo you have in the files in front of you is of a stone I am sure that you have all heard about." There was a rustle of papers as the directors looked at the photo. It was of a very beautiful teardrop ten-carat diamond. They all recognized it as the one that Robert Haverly, the British actor, had given Lady Debra Courtley at their wedding.

"I am sure that all of you read about it in yesterday's Star,*" the Chairman continued dryly, holding the newspaper in his hand. "Even I had to find out about the stone through the local press."*

A titter of laughter ran through the room.

"What the Star *did not write, because they did not know," the Chairman said, looking at the photo in front of him, "is that this stone came from one of our mines. Its signature is that of the Skeleton coast in Namibia. What is even more disconcerting," he continued dramatically, "is that not only were we not aware of its existence, but it passed through our security."*

He leaned back in his chair, pleased at the uproar his statement caused.

"How can this be!" one of the directors demanded. "Is our security so lax that a stone of this size can be so easily stolen?"

"Not at all," the Chairman replied after regaining control of the meeting.

"It is simply that we cannot X-ray each and every worker every day. As you all know, to steal a diamond is simple. Swallow it when no one is looking, hope that you are not in line to be X-rayed, and then wait for it to reappear as nature follows its normal course. At present, we have been X-raying diggers at random, but the trade has become so lucrative, we will have to tighten our surveillance."

"Most definitely. Hear, hear," the table nodded in agreement.

"With this action, we may not be able to stop every smuggler," the Chairman continued, "but at least we can attempt to reduce the number of stones stolen."

"What about tackling it from the other end?" one of the directors asked with a smile. A titter at his pun passed through the room." By this I mean clamping down on the buyers."

"Well," the Chairman replied slowly, "this is exactly the thought I had in mind. I have taken the liberty of employing the services of a retired Scotland Yard detective. He should be able to help us in this regard. In the papers in front of you, you will find his resumé. His name is John Fitzgerald." He paused, waiting for everyone to shuffle through their papers and find the necessary document. He smiled as he saw the numerous nods of agreement as each in turn read the resumé, giving silent approval to his strategy.

"I have instructed the Inspector to find the supply route for the illicit stones from our mines to the cutters in Amsterdam and Israel," he continued. "I believe that if we can seal this route, diggers may be discouraged from stealing, simply because there won't be a market."

"How long do you estimate the investigation will take?" one of the directors interjected.

"I have no idea," the Chairman answered. "I can only say that it could take a number of months or even years. With the board's permission, I would like to give the Inspector authority to travel throughout the world if need be, to find these centers. We have no idea how big the operation is. The only time we know stones are stolen from us is when an IDB dealer is caught and arrested, or when a particularly large stone, like the one in front of you, appears on the market. Admittedly the percentage stolen is small when compared to what we are presently mining, but it increases logarithmically when we compare it to what we release to our buyers."

He looked around the room. "Is there any further comment?" he asked.

"Yes, I have a question."

Everyone turned to look at Reg Sinclair. He was a newly-appointed board member, and was young and ambitious. He had made his way up through the company's ranks into the boardroom by hard work and was considered to be one of South Africa's bright young men. Everyone expected him to one day become chairman of the company.

"Is there no detective in South Africa who can do the job?" he asked. He spoke English slowly with a heavy Afrikaans accent. "Surely someone with knowledge of our country would be better than someone from outside the country."

"We considered this," the Chairman replied, "and we did find a man in South Africa who had an excellent knowledge of the industry. We approached him, but he refused to work with us."

"I have one more question," Reg Sinclair asked. The Chairman looked at him with annoyance. "Who was this South African you felt could have done the job?"

"Brigadier Jan Ellis," the Chairman said brusquely. "He is in charge of the police force guarding the Skeleton Coast in South West Africa."

"Did he give a reason as to why he would not take the assignment?"

The Chairman looked embarrassed. "No, he did not," he replied. "We believe that his decision may have been a political one." Then he said pointedly with a hint of sarcasm in his voice. "He is not very fond of the English," and with that, he adjourned the meeting.

3

JAN AND TOBY WERE BOTH multi-millionaires, but they still lived carefully, not advertising their wealth. The money they received from the sale of the diamonds was carefully hidden in Swiss bank accounts, and whenever they went abroad, they spent lavishly, and brought back into South Africa as much as they felt they could safely smuggle in. They took advantage of the fact that most South Africans, because of the political climate, tried to get money out of the country. No one in their right mind would do the opposite, which was bring money into the country.

In four years Toby had built a huge mansion overlooking the Brakenstroom dam, and Jan had bought the property he wanted in Struisbaai, building a fine house or his retirement. They had both helped their children financially, and both felt very pleased with themselves. Then one day Toby told Jan, "My friend says that it is time we should stop. We have all made enough money, and being greedy could get us into trouble."

Jan agreed, and they stopped. Six months later Jan resigned from the police.

Detective Inspector John Fitzgerald asked for the curtains to be drawn in preparation for the slide presentation.

"Mr. Chairman, gentlemen," he began. "Three years ago you commissioned me to find a smuggling route of illegal diamonds from South Africa to the diamond cutters in Amsterdam and Tel Aviv." As he spoke he projected his first slide onto the screen. "Before I do so," he continued, "I want you all to study this map. This is Kimberley," he pointed at a red dot on the screen, "probably the most famous diamond city in the world. I don't have to tell you that. This area here," and his pointer covered a large area around Kimberley, "is the diamond area from Lichtenberg to Wolmaranstad. Diamonds were spread over the veldt, probably deposited by water many thousands of years ago. This," and he traced a large river south of Lichtenberg, "is the Vaal River. One can only guess at what it holds in its numerous potholes, but I understand that the river is treacherous and protects its treasure."

He paused, looking around the room.

"All of you know this; I don't have to tell you." He turned back to the screen. "This is Johannesburg, and this town," and he pointed to a red dot close to Johannesburg, "is the town that is the pivot point for this vast diamond field. It is also the largest diamond smuggling center in the world."

The directors sat silently, looking at him with disbelief.

"The name of the town," he continued, "is Brakenstroom."

"Inspector," Reg Sinclair said sarcastically as everyone started talking, "I don't doubt your capabilities, but if Brakenstroom is only 100 odd miles from Johannesburg, why did it take you so long and cost us such a great deal of money for you to find this out?"

"Ah," said Fitzgerald to a hushed room as they waited for his answer, "I found it out in the first two weeks I was in South Africa. I then spent the next two and a three-quarter years confirming that there was not a bigger center."

"You solved the problem so easily?" Sinclair persisted.

"It was quite simple, actually," the Inspector replied. "All I did was question six black miners in the three months I was here. The sum of the parcels they had stolen alone added up to a retail value of over a hundred thousand pounds. They had all been arrested in Brakenstroom and had all stolen their diamonds from your workings. Using this as my yardstick, I traveled the world trying to better it. I spoke to hundreds of policemen and prisoners and spent hours looking through thousands of files."

"Who were the stones sold to?"

The inspector looked at the Chairman questioningly.

"This is a closed meeting," the Chairman said, "you can answer the question."

"Well," Fitzgerald said hesitantly, "look amongst the richest of men in South Africa, and even some who don't appear to be that wealthy." He waited for the effect of his words.

"Incidentally," and he started putting his notes together, "in the last three years, a large number of very good stones from South West Africa also found their way to the market. This was unexpected and puzzled me for a while, because your security in the area is exceptionally efficient. Here I must compliment Brigadier Jan Ellis for this efficiency. He has done a sterling job. He personally gave me a guided tour of his security system, and was shocked when I reported my findings to him. I understand that he is retiring in the very near future. Before he does, he assures me that he will tighten security in the area."

The three friends sat on the verandah of Toby's house overlooking the lake. The sun was setting in a huge orange fire-ball and as they looked over the water admiring the beauty, a fish leapt from the surface to catch a fly and the drops of water sparkled like diamonds as it fell back to the lake in a splash.

"Toby," Fitzgerald said, his voice deep with concern, "I hope you and Jan have retired."

Jan smiled. "Fitz, my friend," he said, "that you can be sure of. Toby and I had already made the decision. You know, I was very surprised when Toby told me just the other day that you were our overseas partner. When you came to me in Luderitz, you gave me one hell of a fright."

They all laughed.

"I had to keep Fitz a secret," Toby said, "in much the same way that Fitz never knew that you were involved. You are both policemen. Shows you what a good detective Scotland Yard lost when Fitz retired. Only right at the end did he consider you, and when he confronted me with your identity, I knew that we should stop. It was simply a matter of time before someone else would put two and two together."

"Just tell me," Jan asked Fitzgerald, "what do you owe Toby that made you join us? You are after all a policeman and a good one at that. You have an impeccable record."

Toby looked embarrassed.

"Toby saved my life during the war," Fitzgerald said, looking at Toby. "He picked up a live grenade and threw it. Unfortunately he could not throw it far enough, but he was between me and the explosion, so he took all the blast. His body took so much shrapnel that he nearly died. He still carries some of the metal to this day. When he at first approached me to find a market for illicit diamonds, I nearly refused, but then I thought, what the hell, I am a policeman in Great Britain, not South Africa. Let them take care of their own problems. If and when they should one day ask for help, then I may consider it." They were silent for a while, thinking about what Fitzgerald had said.

"I often wonder," Fitzgerald continued "whether I would have done what Toby did, pick up a live grenade. It is something I hope that I never have to find out." He looked at the two men standing in front of him. "Well, what are the two of you going to do now?" he asked.

"Sannie and I have bought a place at Struisbaai, something we have always wanted," Jan said.

"And Elizabeth and I are taking a world cruise," Toby added. "I think we both need a break. Hopefully when we are in London, we will visit you at your pub. You must tell us where it is."

"There is one for sale in Slough I have put in an offer for," Fitzgerald replied. "If accepted, as soon as everything is finalized and confirmed, I will let you know. Well," he looked at his watch and stood up, "I must be going, I have a plane to catch. I sincerely hope that you will both come and visit me soon."

"But definitely," Jan said as he shook Fitzgerald's hand. "Sannie and I have never been to England. Perhaps it is about time we made our peace. You know, you two Englishmen have changed my life. I must say that we truly had a very good business relationship."

"That we sure did," Toby and Fitzgerald agreed, "that we sure did."

Barney and Pieter

FRIENDSHIP BETWEEN TWO MEN can last a lifetime, but that friendship can be stifled by their wives. Wives either accept their husband's friends and learn to like each other or they make their own friends and expect their husbands to follow them in that new friendship. When forced to accept a woman they do not like because of their husband's friendship, they do so under duress, and their marriage develops stress fractures. If the tension between the wives becomes too great, it is usually the husband who gives in and loses a friend. On the odd occasion, however, the husband does not give in, and interesting stories are usually the result. Brakenstroom, with its diversity of cultures, had a few such stories. One in particular kept the town's tongues wagging for many years.

Barney and Pieter, two men from different religions and different cultures, were friends. The bond between the two men was so great that their wives, when they married, were forced into an uncomfortable social lifestyle. They disliked each other intensely, but Barney and Pieter, who had been friends for as long as either of them could remember, were oblivious to this sintering discord. They were friends and they expected their wives to be friends. The alternative was not even considered.

Barney was David Asher's younger brother. He had been born in Brakenstroom and had attended the local primary and high schools, as did most of the children who spoke English as a home language.

Pieter on the other hand was Afrikaans. His father was a direct descendant of the Voortrekkers who originally came to the Transvaal from the Cape. He was a member of the Dutch Reform Church, and the family practiced their religion with enthusiasm and sincerity. Pieter's mother, on the other hand, had had an English upbringing, and although Afrikaans was their home language, she wanted her son to be bilingual, and for this reason Pieter was sent to an English school.

Barney and Pieter became friends from Grade One, the first class in primary school. They were both six years old and in those days, English- and Afrikaans-speaking children could be sent to the same school, where they learned to respect each other's culture. It was only much later when the National Party came to power that language differences restricted a child to a "Home Language" education.

The two boys went on to matriculate together, dated together, and sometimes even shared the same girlfriend. They virtually lived in each other's house. Even their parents often forgot whose child was whose.

When Barney was barmitzvah'd, Pieter could recite the Portion of the Law as fluently as Barney could. In fact he had attended every chedar class Barney had attended and could not understand why he could not have a Barmitzvah and receive as many presents as Barney did.

Barney, on the other hand, attended Church on a Sunday, although after his Barmitzvah, his sudden Jewish responsibilities made him conscious of the difference between the Dutch Reform Church and the Synagogue.

For seven years the two were separated, when Barney went to the University of the Witwatersrand to study for a Bachelor's Degree in Commerce, and Pieter went to Stellenbosch University to study dentistry. Barney played poker, met and married Marsha, and in the seven years managed to scrape together a B.Com degree. Pieter worked hard at his studies, married Christa who was enjoying University life as a first year student, and qualified with honours as a dentist. Then they both came home, Barney to article as a chartered accountant, and Pieter to a dentistry practice that his father bought for him. Their friendship took up exactly where it left off, as though they had never separated.

Marsha was tall, thin and very lovely, with black curly hair framing an almost patrician face. She carried herself with the air of a woman who knew she was beautiful and dressed accordingly. She was constantly aware of the admiring glances of the men in Brakenstroom, but she dressed for the women, not the men. Men were of little interest to her, not that she had lesbian tendencies, on the contrary, but sex was not her most favourite pastime, something to be avoided as much as possible and tolerated as the "not too pleasant, but bearable" side of a marriage.

Christa was a beauty in a different way, inclined to be slightly overweight. Her jealously of Marsha's slimness made her very mindful of her diet, and with her red-brown hair pulled tightly back into a bun, she presented that reserved dignity that all Afrikaner women do. She dressed for herself, and was lovely in a more comfortable way, with a personality that was pleasant yet vivacious. She attracted as many admiring glances from men as did Marsha, but where Marsha was cool and aloof, Christa enjoyed the company of men and they enjoyed hers. Many men propositioned her and she was flattered by their advances, but the thought of being unfaithful to Pieter never entered her head.

Whenever Marsha and Christa were together in public, they cultivated an outward friendliness that fooled almost everyone except those who knew them more intimately. They both gave birth to two children each, but where Marsha's were girls, Christa's were boys. For all intents and purposes, both women were fully domesticated and part of the Brakenstroom social and tea party scene.

The years passed and it did not take either of them long to become frustrated with the smallness of Brakenstroom, because after all, Marsha was a Johannesburg girl while Christa had come from Cape Town. They both found the narrow-mindedness of a small country town stifling. Marsha continually bemoaned her fate and spent more and more time in Johannesburg "shopping" as she called it, while Christa would find any excuse to visit her parents in Cape Town.

Over the years, Barney had qualified as a chartered accountant and had built a small but profitable accounting practice, while Pieter became a very successful dentist, taking in two partners. Barney looked more and more to playing poker for entertainment, while Pieter started to drown his sorrows, the few he could find, with acquaintances after a game of golf at "The Club." They spoke to each other every day, and spent almost every weekend together, either playing golf, or barbecuing at the yacht club, or simply relaxing at a pool at either one of their houses. Their wives had no alternative but to fall in with their husband's lifestyle. They brought up their children according to their respective cultures and put up with each other's company only because of their husbands, who were too involved in themselves to notice the tension that was gradually developing. Life was uncomplicated but extremely boring, causing both men to look for something more exciting.

What they eventually became involved in was IDB, (Illicit Diamond Buying). Brakenstroom was the center of the diamond diggings in South Africa, with uncut diamonds coming to the town from Kimberley and Lichtenburg. Parcels offered were small and could easily be disposed of in Johannesburg. Almost anyone in Brakenstroom who was presented with the opportunity had tried their hand at it some time or other, so it was natural that the two friends should also try their luck, as they put it. The only risk and humiliation was to be caught, and that made the game even more exciting.

Marsha and Christa were aware of their husband's illegal business, but they simply turned a blind eye and ignored the whispers and snide remarks that soon started among the gossip mongers of Brakenstroom.

"I mean," they would console themselves, "there are two honest dishonesties. The one is cheating the Receiver of Revenue, and the other is IDB," and everyone in Brakenstroom would have agreed with them.

The way Pieter and Barney ran their operation was very simple. Barney, with a 50% capital investment from Pieter, bought a small jewelry store in the town. Pieter then bought the stones from the various Africans that worked on the mines in the area, and gave them to Barney who 'fenced' them in Johannesburg. With the connections Barney developed in the jewelry trade, he had a ready and very confidential market. Neither Pieter nor Barney ever considered themselves to be criminals. They felt that they were just shrewd businessmen outwitting the law, and at the same time enjoying the danger that came with it.

Unfortunately, all good things must eventually come to an end. The partnership started developing stress fractures when one day Christa decided that Pieter had taken a fancy to Marsha, simply because he had started sleeping off his beer drinking sessions, rather than giving her the sexual attention she needed. She was not oversexed, but she did enjoy her lovemaking. She looked around for an excuse, and there was Marsha. It was a bad choice, because Marsha, as we know, was cool, cold, and not that interested in sex. If anyone had had the courage to ask Barney over a couple of glasses of Scotch what she was like in bed, he would have probably answered, "Nothing to talk about, quite frigid. She lies there like a board, and I have to do all the work . . . with little satisfaction."

However, he never did talk much about Marsha, because being her husband gave him a degree of status. He saw admiration for her beauty in the eyes of other men and this gave him a quiet satisfaction. He drowned his sex problems by joining a gym and found that the daily work-out quelled his frustrations. Sexual satisfaction when he needed it came from his persistence, when Marsha would eventually allow him to touch her as she lay motionless on the bed, not participating at all while he deftly brought her to orgasm as he came to his.

"Like animals," she muttered once.

"Is the problem with me?" he asked her.

She shook her head. "No."

"Then what is the problem?" he persisted, feeling sorry for himself.

"I don't know," and, turning her back to him, that was the end of that.

"Why not see a psychiatrist?" he would plead.

"Okay," she would answer softly, but she never ever saw one. It was far easier to agree with him than to argue with him.

Eventually, even trying to make love to her had become too much of an effort, so he simply stopped. He would always love her, but the constant thought that her frigidity could be because he was a bad lover made him turn to celibacy. He was ripe for an affair but did not know it. All that was needed was for someone to reel him in.

Pieter and Barney made a good living out of their professions, and IDB was the cherry on the cake. They were exceptionally cautious, not displaying too much wealth in Brakenstroom, but living it up when they could, away from the town. They soon established contacts in Israel and Amsterdam, and began to take overseas trips together, at least once a year. On all these trips, Christa kept a watchful eye on Pieter, trying to catch him red-handed with Marsha.

This lifestyle went on for about two years and by all accounts they should have been content with their very comfortable style of living, but the two men were always looking for "the BIG one," as Pieter used to say, "the one that will keep all four wheels on the wagon."

The opportunity presented itself one day when both men went on a lion hunting expedition to the Kalahari. The idea was to fly to Gaberone in Botswana and then to travel by Landrover into the desert.

Gaberone is the capital of Botswana, and sported a casino at one of the local hotels, an attraction to many South Africans who enjoyed the tables, the strip shows, and the black prostitutes. The other attraction, the enormous game reserves in the north of the country, were sporting some of the largest herds of game on the African continent. Botswana was also the home of the Okavango waterway flowing into a sea of sand to form the swamp, a tourist's delight with its teeming herds of game.

When diamonds were discovered at Orapa, Botswana, once one of the poorest countries, soon became one of the richest countries per capita in the world.

On this particular safari, Pieter was approached and offered a parcel of uncut stones. This could easily have been a trap, so after talking to Barney he turned down the offer, telling the seller that he had no money. He did inform him that he would be back in a month's time, and if the seller was still interested, he would look at a possible purchase.

Their hunt was now spoiled, because instead of concentrating on lions, they spent their days scheming as to how they would buy the parcel and get away with it. By the time they returned to Brakenstroom, of course without a lion, Pieter had worked out a plan, and he put it to Barney.

"Man," he said with a beer in his hand, walking up and down the lounge of his house as he spoke, "it is so bloody easy."

Barney sat in an easy chair sipping a Scotch on ice and waited. He knew his friend and he knew his plans, and he knew that they usually worked.

"You must go down two days before me on a business trip," Pieter continued. "Book into the room next to me, and I will come later, on a hunting trip. I will arrange to meet the Ou (person), inspect the stones, and once a price has been established, take them to the safe in the bedroom to collect the money. You will have come in through the inter-leading door and hidden in the bathroom. I will give you the parcel and you will quickly go back to your room, lock the door, and if there is a raid on my room, then no stones will be found. You will have them."

Barney thought for a few minutes then asked, "What about trying the Houdini trick?"

"The what trick?" Pieter looked at Barney as he sat sipping his whisky, a sly smile on his face.

"The Houdini trick," Barney repeated.

"What is that, man?" Pieter asked, irritated that his friend should query his idea.

Barney swirled his whisky in the glass, enjoying the tinkle of the ice cubes. Pieter waited impatiently while he sorted out his thoughts.

"Houdini was a famous magician," he said eventually, "who worked out many tricks, with his wife as an accomplice. One of them was the famous 'Houdini trick.' "

"So," Pieter asked derisively as he drank his beer. "What is this Houdini trick then, hey?"

"Well," Barney replied, sitting forward in his chair, "I will take the room next door, but not on the same floor. I will take the room directly above you. In the afternoon, we will connect a piece of elastic, the type we used to make ketties (catapults or slingshots) with, between the balconies of both rooms. The elastic will be stretched, tight. Your side will have a clip, like the one on your hunting belt. When you get the parcel, you put it in a small flour bag, close it with a safety pin, and then clip the hook to the safety pin. All you have to do is let it go, and it will vanish into the dark. I will reel it in upstairs."

Pieter thought for a moment. "Maar jy is n slim Jood (But you are a clever Jew), it is very clever," Pieter laughed, and poured Barney another Scotch. "I have always said that there is nothing in this world more clever than the brains of a Jew and an Afrikaner when they work together."

They both laughed. Barney was pleased that Pieter had accepted his idea. The last few months he had felt that their friendship had become a bit strained and he did not know why. For the first time in years Pieter and Christa had actually missed a few Sundays with them, Christa saying that they had to attend Nagmaal, (Holy Communion), for the sake of their children.

The next day he and Pieter practiced the Houdini trick until they perfected it. They even went on a dummy run to Gaberone and it worked beautifully. Now all they had to do was phone the contact.

A week later the deal was set. As an extra precaution, Barney drove to Gaberone while Pieter flew. Everything worked exactly as planned. There was no trap, but they were happy with the precaution they took.

"It is never the first one," Pieter said to Barney as they celebrated their success later the same evening, "it is on the second or third one that they trap you. This first one is the bait, by the third one, you are careless. Where have you hidden the stones?"

"In the radiator of the car," Barney replied nonchalantly.

Pieter absorbed his statement for a few minutes. "Now that *is* clever," he said with admiration, "no one will think of looking there."

The next morning, Barney drove back to Brakenstroom.

The parcel of uncut diamonds was bigger than any parcel they had had before. In fact, it was the equivalent of twelve of their normal parcels. Soon, they were visiting Botswana every three to four months. The parcels were gradually getting larger and they were becoming very wealthy men.

Barney and Marsha bought a second house in Johannesburg, where they spent every weekend, although as time passed, Marsha spent less and less time during the week in Brakenstroom, because she insisted that the girls should have a Jewish schooling at the King David school in Johannesburg.

Pieter and Christa bought a second home in Hermanus. With the twin propeller Beechcraft airplane that Pieter had learned to fly, they would travel down for any and every long weekend that was on the calendar.

The friendship between the two men gradually drifted further apart and they spent less and less time in each other's company. Their wives and their family commitments were more demanding of their time and although they saw each other during the week, or whenever they had a deal on the go, weekends were now spent with their respective families, away from each other. But with all the extra comfort and luxury, both wives were still not happy.

"Pieter," Christa would constantly nag him, "you are getting fat with all that beer you are drinking. You must start losing weight."

He in turn would try to kiss her and she would accept his beer-smelling kisses, but his attempts at lovemaking no longer satisfied her.

Marsha, on the other hand, simply never allowed Barney to touch her, and Barney hoping that Marsha would one day start giving him her favours, spent even more time at gym. He lost weight and became very fit, running in the Comrades marathon and finishing well enough to earn a silver medal.

Christa started to compare Pieter to Barney more and more. Her jealousy of Marsha started to focus on Barney. She became sarcastic and antagonistic on the few occasions Barney visited them at their home, making him feel unwelcome, deliberately preparing unsavory meals to discourage him further.

"For God's sake," Pieter shouted at her one evening, after Barney had left. "Couldn't you have prepared a better meal than that?"

"If you don't like my food, then you know what to do!" she retorted. "You can't expect me to prepare a decent meal at a moment's notice."

Pieter's eyes narrowed slightly. "But at least try and give him something decent to eat," he retorted. "The bitch he is married to gives him nothing. No food, no sex, no family life. She lives in Joh'burg and he lives here. No wonder the poor bugger spends so much time at the gym eyeing all those sexy girls in their leotards. Why the hell he doesn't divorce her I don't know."

"Barney told you this?" Christa asked, curious to find out more about Marsha. "When did he tell you all this?"

"One night at the club," Pieter answered, opening another beer. "He was feeling quite down, so he let it all out. He told me that one of the girls at the gym made a pass at him, and the idiot did not realize that she had until much later."

"And what did you tell him?" Christa asked, fascinated.

"Oh I told him to always take a little bit of tail, especially when it is offered to you on a plate."

"Oh you did, did you?" Christa said, amused. "I suppose that is exactly what you would do."

"Well," Pieter said, looking at her slyly, "if you ever held out on me, I would feel tempted."

"Go for it," she said cooly. "Go for it before that big boep [beer belly] of yours gets in the way." She walked from the room muttering to herself while he chuckled.

Her curiosity was aroused. She started to look at Barney with new eyes and she soon saw that other women did indeed find him attractive. She began to think of him no longer as Marsha's husband but as someone who appealed to women. The next time he came to dinner she prepared an exceptional meal, and made a point of talking to him and listening to him when he spoke. She was amazed at his charm and surprised how, over the years, he had developed a sophistication and worldliness that her husband lacked. She enjoyed the evening immensely, surprised that she had never noticed the change in him before. Pieter watched her closely throughout the evening, puzzled.

"What the devil are you up to?" he asked her when Barney left.

"You told me to be nice to him, so I am," she remarked flippantly.

"Watch it liefie, [darling]," he warned her, "you are playing with fire. He is a man who is like a spring. He needs a woman badly, and it won't be you. I am warning you." She laughed at him as she walked into the kitchen and did not see the anger in his eyes.

She started looking forward to seeing Barney more and more and it was now she, not Pieter who invited him to dinner. She made sure that he arrived at least half an hour before Pieter came home from work so that she could be alone with him. She found that she enjoyed his company and knew that because of his and Pieter's friendship, his visits would not attract the attention of the local gossips. She gradually forgot her original plan, which was to make Pieter jealous and so lose weight. Had anyone told her that she was falling in love with Barney, she would have laughed at the idea. He was her husband's friend and business partner. That was all there was to it.

Once a year, the local women organized a dance to raise funds for the Brakenstroom orphanage. The dance was the event of the year, very formal, and very, very select. Tickets were R100 each, and only 100 tickets were sold. Only the cream of Brakenstroom society attended, and then usually only those who danced.

Christa, as she had done every year in the past, had organized a table that included Barney and Marsha. This year, though, she made sure that she sat directly opposite Barney, so that she could look at him and talk to him. She had spent a great deal of money on herself, and her dress was a very expensive creation from Paris,

France that cunningly highlighted her physical beauty. She wanted to look ravishing, and she did and she knew it.

"She is like a cheap hussy tonight," Marsha whispered to Barney. "That dress of hers is disgusting." She stood up, taking his hand, knowing that Christa was watching her. She was proud of the fact that Barney looked so handsome in his tuxedo, whereas Pieter looked gross in his growing obesity.

"Don't hold me so close," she commanded as they danced. "You will crush my corsage." They danced like robots without saying another word to each other.

Pieter was his ebullient self, cracking jokes and rapidly becoming drunk on the fine red wine at the table. He was a poor dancer and usually spent his evening moving from table to table, drinking and joking with his friends. He had outgrown his tuxedo, which was stretched to the limit across his waist. It wasn't long before his shirt was sopping wet with perspiration. Christa was disgusted with him and instead of joining him as he moved around the hall, sat in a sulk at the table sipping more wine than she normally did, refusing the numerous invitations to dance.

When Barney eventually asked her, as was customary, she was more than slightly drunk. Moving into Barney's arms on the dance floor, she felt comfortable and started dancing very close to him. She knew that he was a good dancer and so was she. When the band stopped playing, instead of allowing him to take her back to her table as he usually did after one dance, she held his hand and moved into his arms for another dance. He was surprised; this was not like Christa. At previous dances she usually danced with almost every man in the room and only kept one perfunctory dance for him.

Tonight, instead of simply dancing, Christa moved in very close, enjoying Barney's strength and body contact. She put her cheek against his and pressed her hips to his so that his right leg as they danced was always between hers, against her groin.

Their first dance had aroused him. By the time the second dance came to an end, he had an extremely hard and painful erection. Christa had danced so close to him that he had felt her firm nipples through the front of his shirt and this had excited him even more.

When after five dances they eventually left the floor, not because they wanted to, but because the band had taken their customary break, they were both well and truly on edge. He led

Christa to the table and as he sat down he noticed the slight frown on Marsha's face.

"Christa just felt like dancing," he whispered as an excuse, mopping the sweat off his forehead.

"You look a mess," Marsha whispered cooly. "You are sopping wet. Don't leave me alone again."

He gulped his wine and then nearly choked as he felt a foot curl up in his crotch. He looked at Christa sitting opposite him, amazement on his face. She was talking to Pieter as though nothing was happening. Then, glancing in his direction, she gave a sly smile and started telling Marsha how much she enjoyed the band. He tried to compose himself, but when Christa started rubbing her foot from side to side, he jumped up.

"What is wrong with you tonight?" Marsha asked irritably. "You simply cannot sit still."

"It's hot in here," he replied. He looked at Christa then back at Marsha and mumbled, hurrying to get away.

"I am going outside for a second, to get a drink, can I get you anything?" and without even waiting for an answer, he rushed from the table.

The air was cool after the heat of the hall. He gulped it in, enjoying its cold crispness. He walked through the car park to his car, his wet shirt clinging coldly to his body. He sat on the back seat of the car and leaned back closing his eyes, his thoughts in a turmoil.

There was a knock on the window and he looked up. Christa was leaning forward to attract his attention, her breasts revealed as the front of her dress gaped open. His pulse quickened. Without questioning his actions further, he opened the door. She climbed into the car, moving into his embrace.

They made love as though it were for the first time, fumbling and uncertain of each other. They made love as though they were two teenagers, exploring each other's bodies and delighting in their new-found experience. They made love, and it seemed to go on forever, and when they had both climaxed, the world started moving again, the fireworks vanished from the night.

Barney lay exhausted with Christa in his arms. "You are wonderful," he whispered into her ear.

"You are more than wonderful," she replied as she nestled her head against his chest, sleepy from the warm glow of their lovemaking.

For Barney, those words were what he needed to hear. All his fears of being a poor lover melted away.

"I think I love you, Christa," he said, and as he said it, he realized that he meant it. "I think I have loved you for a very long time and did not know it."

She smiled contentedly in his arms.

This was the start of their affair. Barney's sexual fantasies were satisfied and Christa, with every pelvic thrust, felt her anger toward Pieter justified. Having an affair worried her at first, as it broke her sacred vows of marriage, but a few of her golfing friends had had the odd one-night-stand with a golfer, so she consoled herself with the belief that her affair with Barney would not last very long. The one friend she did confide in, agreed with her that it was simply a matter of making Pieter jealous, not that she loved Barney, oh no, she was simply using Barney until Pieter lost weight and started looking after himself. Then she would break it off and she and Pieter would lead a happily married life.

Marsha never queried the fact that Barney stopped troubling her in bed. She had started leading an active social life in Johannesburg and any suspicions she may have had, she put aside. She counted her blessings and not having to have sex, was one of them.

Pieter, on the other hand, demanded his rights, usually once a week. Christa satisfied them, but without the fire that she had previously given. This she reserved for Barney, who was clay in her hands. Pieter suspected nothing.

On the first anniversary of the start of their relationship, Barney gave Christa a diamond bracelet. Christa had come to Johannesburg and had booked into the Sandton Sun hotel. Barney joined her, having told Marsha that he would be on a business trip. He was like a love-sick bull continually scheming how he could be with Christa. She enjoyed his attention and in a perverse sort of way, the power she held over the husband of Marsha.

The bracelet he gave her was magnificent. He had chosen each and every stone with care and had designed it himself. It was worth a small fortune, but he and Pieter were doing so well that he could afford it.

Christa showed her appreciation in ways Barney had never thought was possible. Now came the problem. How was she to get the bracelet back to Brakenstroom without having Pieter ask too many questions? Pieter always gave her plenty of money, but not enough to buy such a lavish gift. After a great deal of thought, she hit on the idea of locking it in a 'left luggage cage' at the Johannesburg Railway Station. She would tell Pieter that she had picked up "this key" which belonged to the cage, and that finders were keepers.

She very carefully wrapped the bracelet in old newspaper, placed it in a shoe box, and drove to the station. Renting one of the cages, she carefully placed the shoe box tied with string at the bottom of the cage, and heaped some old newspapers on top of it, a deterrent to anyone who may possibly burgle the cage. Then she drove home, planning the story she would tell Pieter.

"Keep it short and simple," she eventually decided, "then you can never be caught out in a lie."

When she told Pieter the story of the key, and how she had found it, she was shaking. Pieter believed her and much to her delight even offered to check the cage the very next day, as he would be in Johannesburg on business.

"Whatever is there, is yours," he said, as she handed him the key.

The day was a long one for her as she waited in eager anticipation, proud of herself for having thought up such a clever scheme.

When Pieter eventually returned late that night, she forced herself to sit calmly in the lounge, waiting for him to come into the house. Eventually she could wait no more. He was taking far too long to park the car. She stood up, walked to the door, opened it, and called out to him in the dark.

"Pieter, is that you?"

"Ja liefie (Yes darling)," he answered.

"Did you get the shoe box?" she shouted, and then immediately regretted her impulsiveness. Surely he would query her knowledge that it was a shoe box?

His answer took some time in coming. "Yes," he eventually called back, "I did find an old shoe box."

After what seemed an eternity he walked in, giving her a perfunctory kiss on the cheek. She kissed him back expecting him to hand her the shoe box, but he was carrying only his briefcase. She seethed, but brought herself under control. He walked to the bar and opened a beer.

"Would you like a drink?" he asked.

"No thank you," she replied, and then unable to contain herself blurted out, "Where is it?"

"Where is what?" he asked. "Oh, you mean the shoe box. Ach yes, it is in the back of the car."

She stood up. "Give me your car keys," she said, angry at the fact that he was so casual. "I will go and get it".

He gave her the keys and sat down in the armchair, enjoying his beer.

After a few minutes she returned with the shoe box in her hand.

"Is this what you found?" she asked, trying to stay as calm as possible. "It looks like an ordinary shoe box. I wonder what is inside?"

"Hell," Pieter muttered into his beer. "I don't know. I just took the box and left."

She put the box on the table and untied the string. She took the lid off expecting to see the black satin holder of the bracelet. Instead, she saw a pair of dirty old shoes.

"What . . . . what . . . ." she started spluttering.

"Is something wrong, my dear?" Pieter asked, sipping his beer.

She looked at him, shock etched on her face.

"No . . . . no . . . ." she mumbled, feeling sick.

"Oh, I thought there may have been." He threw his head back and emptied the beer mug. Wiping the foam from his mouth with the back of his hand as he stood up, he walked to the door of the lounge. Turning towards her he belched loudly and said, "I am so tired. I really had a hard but a very profitable day in Johannesburg, very profitable indeed. I think I will go to bed." As he turned to walk to the bedroom, he paused looked slyly at her as she stood pondering the shoe box on the table.

"You were right, my darling, finders are keepers. Coming?" and he belched again with great gusto.

Christa was devastated at the loss of the bracelet. Where she had simply tolerated Pieter before and hoped he would change, she now started to hate him. Her attitude towards him became brusque, and she could not bear to be alone with him. Where before she was a faithful, happy, God-fearing Afrikaner wife, she now considered herself to be a fallen woman simply because her affair was obviously no longer a secret from him. What upset her more than anything else was that he had outwitted her. She still attended church with the children regularly every Sunday morning, but she felt that God had somehow forsaken her. She was on her own.

Barney was continually in her thoughts, and she began to realize that she had fallen deeply in love with him. He had brought out emotions in her that she never knew were there, emotions that, after a year of being his mistress, still frightened her.

The thought that Pieter, who became fatter and more slovenly in both his looks and manner, was still her husband made her determined to hurt him and hurt him where he would not recover. She started paying an interest in everything he did. She watched and waited and remained the respectful wife, never mentioning the bracelet, although Barney did ask her every now and then why she never wore it. She simply told him that it was too dangerous to wear openly at the moment.

Barney and Pieter remained friends, but their friendship was dying. Pieter was not sure who his wife's lover was and became suspicious of anyone who looked twice at Christa. They spent less and less time in each other's company, only seeing each other when they had a business deal. Barney seldom came to dinner, as he and Christa were scared that by being together in front of Pieter, they may give the game away. They still saw each other every day, usually at gym, early in the morning when there were few people present. On the odd morning Barney would meet her somewhere in town, or they would drive into the countryside and spend hours walking and talking. They were deeply in love, and their love gave them that friendship only found among lovers.

It was almost six months later that the opportunity Christa was waiting for came. She and Barney had found a quiet hotel at Muldersdrift, close to Johannesburg. They usually met there once a week, more often if they could. They had made passionate love, and he lay in bed watching her as she strapped on her bra, enjoying the sight of her full breasts as she confined them in her brassiere.

"I can't make it next week," he said.

She pulled her dress over her head and stood in front of the mirror, smoothing it over her hips with the palms of her hands, admiring her flat tummy.

"Why not?" she asked looking at him in the mirror as he lay on the bed totally nude. She enjoyed looking at him. His body was lean and hard, not over-developed as other body-builders, but slim and sinuous. She felt herself warming to him, and looked away. She was curious. The only time they had missed any previous rendezvous was when Marsha had wanted Barney to join her on a holiday.

"Pieter and I are doing a big one this time," he explained as he sat up in bed. "Abdul phoned in and said he had a R5 million parcel and that we should go for it." Abdul was their contact in Gaberone.

"Why so big?" she asked as she sat down at the dressing table, her lipstick in her hand.

"Well, he wants to emigrate to Canada," Barney replied. "All his kids are there, and he feels that he has made enough over the years." Then, as an afterthought, "You know, Abdul is almost seventy. I suppose it is time for Pieter and I to stop as well. We have made plenty and have been lucky enough not to have been caught. There is no point in tempting fate."

Christa's mind raced ahead. Here was a way she could get her revenge on Pieter. She knew their routine; it never changed. And although once or twice Barney's car had been searched, the officers at customs had never thought of draining the radiator.

She smiled to herself. The plan she had thought of was so simple, she would . . .

"I will come with both of you this time," she said carefully choosing her words so that her excitement did not show. "We will make a weekend of it."

Barney was pleased. On trips like this, after a purchase had been made, Pieter usually became drunk and gambled 'til the early hours of the morning. Marsha never came with them as she hated Gaberone. A weekend with Christa would be wonderful.

Christa was excited. There was not much time to put her plan into action, so she had to move very fast. She spent the next four days in Johannesburg and Pretoria . Everything fell perfectly into place. Then she told Pieter that she and the children were joining him in Gaberone.

"Why?" he asked. "Why all of a sudden now, this time. All the other times you said that you hated Gaberone. Why must you come this time?" He was irritated, because the size of the parcel was putting pressure on him. "Can't you stay at home?"

"No," she said vehemently, " I want to come with you. It is a long time since I have been in Gaberone, and a weekend to simply relax in the sun is what I need. To be quite honest,"she lied, "I am arranging a trip for myself and the boys to the Okavongo Delta; I have always wanted to go. The guide, Chris van Lonkhuizen, will be in Gaberone, and we have arranged to meet and plan the trip. If you want to join us . . ." she tentatively made the offer.

When the day arrived, she and the two boys flew with Pieter, while Barney, as usual, went by car. By now the staff at the hotel knew them, and they always received a warm welcome. They were big tipsters, and Pieter especially enjoyed the casino. The two men no longer used the Houdini trick, as Abdul had become a trusted friend, but caution always prevailed.

The drop and the subsequent payment occurred exactly as planned. When Barney returned to his room with the stones, Christa was waiting for him in a negligee. A bottle of champagne with two glasses stood on the table beside the bed.

He closed the door quickly behind him and took her into his arms. He kissed her passionately.

"Not yet," she said, pushing him away gently. "Don't you have to hide something first?"

"It can wait a while," he said impatiently.

"Show me what they look like," she asked, patting the bed next to her. "I have never seen an uncut stone."

He took a little chamois leather bag out of his inside pocket. It was full of uncut diamonds. He opened the draw-string, made a depression on the bedspread with his hand, and poured them out in front of her.

"But they look like pieces of dirty glass," she said, holding one up to the light.

He smiled. "Wait until they are cut," he said. "Then they are beautiful, almost as good as those on your bracelet." She ignored the jab.

He walked around the room, restlessly. He wanted her so badly, especially now. Her flimsy negligee hid very little, and one breast escaped as she leaned forward to look at each stone. He started undressing.

"There are a lot of good ones here," he said, opening the bottle of champagne. "Abdul must have kept the best out of every previous parcel he sold us. If he's given us this, I would love to see what he intends to take out with him."

"What are they worth?" she asked, starting to put them back into the pouch.

"On the retail market, they should cut to about R20 to R30 million. We should get about R10 million for them, perhaps a little more, a little less."

She nodded, deep in thought. She lifted each of the bigger stones, looked at it in the ligh,t and placed it carefully in the pouch. Then she took a handful of the smaller stones and let them run from her hand, enjoying their feel as they fell to the bed. She then poured them into the pouch, pulling the strings to close the mouth. She placed the pouch on the dresser beside her, and reached for the glass of champagne he held out to her.

"Barney my love," she whispered as she took the glass from him, "just remember that I love you dearly, and I always will." She held the glass towards him as though in a toast, drank from it, then switched off the light, and pulled him towards her on the bed. They made passionate love. He was more than pleased, because tonight she made love to him and she was insatiable.

He slept with her in his arms, his hand cupping her breast, very contented and happy. He felt her move, and she whispered, "I have to visit the bathroom." After what seemed like an eternity, she returned to his arms, and she made love to him again.

At about 3 a.m. he woke and then woke her.

"You had better go back to your room," he whispered. "The casino will close soon. I must also visit my car."

She yawned, stretched, and slipped on her gown.

"See you in Brakenstroom," he told her, and he held her close.

She took him by the shoulders, looked into his eyes, then kissed him passionately.

"Good-bye, my love," she whispered as she slipped out of his arms, and then, so softly that he did not hear her, "Yes we will see each other, but hopefully not in Brakenstroom. Thank you," she said louder and, blowing him a kiss, she slipped through the door, closing it softly behind her.

He smiled, pleased with himself. Picking up the pouch, he waited a few minutes, then left the room, going to his car. When he came back after pouring the stones into the radiator, he crawled back into bed. The bed was still warm where she had slept and he could smell her body odor faintly on the sheets. He was pleased and he slept well.

The next morning he had breakfast early without seeing Pieter, who usually flew out of Gaberone in the afternoon. He waited a while, hoping to see Christa, but she did not appear. He then paid his bill.

"Sir," the concierge said, "this letter is for you."

Barney looked at the envelope. It was addressed to him in Christa's handwriting. He opened it and read.

"When you get home, go to Oom Piet at the clubhouse. He will give you a letter marked 'Private and Confidential.' Please read it and I hope you follow its instructions. I am sorry, but I had to do it. One day I will tell you why. I hope you will join me and the boys. I love you far too much for you not to come."

He frowned, read it a second time and looked at the concierge.

"The lady who gave this to you?" he asked, holding up the letter.

"She checked out early this morning with her two sons," the porter replied.

"Do you know where she went?"

"She caught a cab to the airport, sir."

"Thank you," Barney said, puzzled by Christa's actions. He collected his luggage, paid his bill, and drove back to Brakenstroom. "I wonder why she left before Pieter?" he mused.

That night, as he drove up the driveway to the garage at Pieter's house, he saw that Pieter was waiting for him.

"What took you so bloody long. . ." Pieter shouted at him.

Barney was puzzled. It was usual for Pieter to wait for him so that they could tap the radiator the same night and recover the diamonds, but he never waited outside the house, nor was he ever this agitated.

". . . and did you give Christa a good-night kiss?"

The blood drained from Barney's face. "What are you talking about?" he asked, trying not to show his concern.

"Look, man, do you think I am blind? The way you two kept looking at each other," and Pieter shook his head angrily in frustration. "Hell, man, I knew she had a lover, but you? I have been a fucking idiot, and last night, when she didn't sleep in our room . . ." He walked angrily up and down as Barney stood watching him, not knowing what to say or do. Then Pieter stopped in front of him and shouted, the spittle of his anger spraying into Barney's face. "Why the hell did you bring them back with you? Where is she?" and he rushed to the car peering angrily inside, expecting to see

Christa and his two sons. "What have you done with them?" he shouted when he saw they were not in the car.

"What do you mean by 'bring her back with me?" Barney asked. "I didn't bring them with me. The concierge told me that Christa and the boys took a cab to the airport."

Barney forced himself to remain calm. Pieter angry was bad, but Pieter drunk and angry was someone to be scared of, and Pieter was very drunk.

"What is going on?" Barney asked, puzzled at Pieter's anger. "I thought Christa and the boys flew back ahead of you."

"That bloody bitch," Pieter shouted. "This note was stuck on the mirror of the bathroom at the hotel." He threw a piece of paper at Barney. Barney bent down and picked it up. He moved to the light of the veranda and read it. It was written in Afrikaans.

"Thank you, Pieter," he read, *"for what you have given me. I am just sorry that I had to take it from Barney as well, but he can reclaim his share if he wants to. Don't try to find me and the children, because our first stop is London, and after that, a new life, and a good one at that, thanks to both of you. By the way,* FINDERS KEEPERS, *although mine was more of a swap. Houdini had more tricks up his sleeve than just one. It's amazing how sugar crystals look like uncut diamonds in the moonlight. Don't blame Barney. He didn't know."*

Barney looked up from the note in astonishment.

"My God, " he whispered to himself, "so that's what it was all about." He remembered the champagne and the way Christa had made love to him, insatiably. She must have switched the diamonds when she went to the bathroom.

"What the fuck does she mean by sugar crystals?" Pieter swore. "And what does she mean by 'you can reclaim your share if you want to.' Did she see the stones? Was she in your fucking room last night?" He grabbed Barney by his lapels and shook him, "Were you fucking my wife?" He spat at Barney. "Come on man," he shouted as he pushed Barney away from him, "let's strip the bloody radiator and find out where those diamonds are."

The two men worked at a frenzy all night, but not one stone was found. Pieter, his anger uncontrollable, walked into the house. He took his sjambok (leather whip tipped with steel) from his study, and while Barney was still working on the car, started whipping him.

"You fucking bastard," he screamed, the sjambok whistling in his hand, "not only were you fucking my wife, but you have stolen my diamonds."

The pain of the whipping made Barney swing around and try to grab at the sjambok with his right hand while his left hand protected his eyes. Pieter danced out of his reach and kept whipping him, trapping him in the corner of the garage. Barney sank to his knees in pain and as he did so, Pieter stepped in and hit him a tremendous blow to the jaw with the wooden leather-wrapped handle of the sjambok. With Pieter's weight behind the blow, Barney never had a chance. He didn't feel Pieter kick him savagely as he fell. He also didn't see the neighbours, who rushed to help after hearing his screams. He recovered consciousness in hospital five days later, with a broken jaw and a few broken ribs, one of which had pierced a lung, and a body bruised and raw with welts from the whip. When Pieter had punched him, his head had fallen back onto the cement floor and he had suffered such a severe concussion that the doctors, fearing for his life, had flown him to a Johannesburg hospital.

While he was recovering, Marsha closed up and sold the house in Brakenstroom, pleased that she was finally severing her ties with a town she disliked.

"Uh, good afternoon, Mrs Asher." Oom Piet, the barman at the golf club tipped his hat to her as she stood before her car preparing to leave. "I heard that you were in town."

"Yes, Oom Piet," Marsha said impatiently, standing at the door to her car. The moving truck with the last of the furniture had already left, and she wanted to arrive in Johannesburg before the movers did so that she could supervise the unloading.

"Uh, this letter was given to me by Christa Henning for your husband. He was supposed to collect it, but I suppose with the accident and all, he can't. Would you please give it to him?" He handed Marsha a letter addressed to Barney marked, "Private & Confidential."

"Certainly, Oom Piet, " she said, "but please excuse me, I have a long way to drive, and I should get going."

"Yes, ma'am," Oom Piet said, raising his hand to his hat in a farewell gesture, "and please give Barney my best wishes, and I hope he recovers soon." He turned and walked away. He had never liked Marsha and her dismissal of him made him like her even less.

Marsha looked at the letter. Her curiosity got the better of her. She opened it and read it. On reaching Johannesburg, she drove directly to her lawyer and started divorce proceedings.

When Barney eventually left the hospital, it was his brother David who collected him. Marsha had packed all his clothes and sent them to David's house. She did not want to see him again. He was devastated, but was too tired and confused to fight her. That night, when he unpacked his suitcase, he found a letter neatly placed on top of his clothes. It was addressed to him and marked, "Private & Confidential." He saw that it had been opened. He read it, smiled, looked at the plane ticket that was in the envelope, and saw that it was still valid. The reason for Marsha divorcing him so abruptly was now clear. He was grateful to her for at least giving him the letter.

He never brought a case of assault against Pieter. He simply sold his business and vanished to become one more Brakenstroom story to be told at the club.

"Remember," people would say, nodding their heads knowingly, "oil and water cannot be mixed. An Afrikaner is an Afrikaner, an Englishman is an Englishman, and a Jew is a Jew. Stay with your Church and stay with your kind."

Pieter stayed on in Brakenstroom. He divorced Christa, remarried, and slowly regained the town's respect, eventually becoming a town councillor. Although he tried to become Mayor, and a few times came close to being elected, he always lost the final vote, much to his disappointment. He never lost weight, and a week before his sixtieth birthday, he had a fatal heart attack. His new wife, Hettie, in sorting through his papers in his safe, found a beautiful diamond bracelet. She wondered why Pieter had never given it to her. She started wearing it on important occasions, and her friends remarked on its exquisite beauty.

Twelve years later, one of the younger club members told how, while on a visit to Vancouver, Canada, he had met a couple who used to live in Brakenstroom.

"Their names were Barney and Christa Asher," he said to Oom Piet. "They told me that if I should see you, I should give you their regards."

"You must mean Barney and Marsha Asher," Oom Piet remarked from behind the bar.

"No, no, I know he said Christa. Although she spoke to me in English with a Canadian accent, she must have been Afrikaans-speaking at one time, because she tested her Afrikaans on me. She was still quite fluent."

"What did she look like?" Oom Piet asked curiously.

"Lets see, she was about five foot five, rather plump with reddish hair. She was full of beans, always laughing and joking."

"Are you sure she was his wife?"

"Oh, yes," he answered, "Barney definitely introduced her to me as his wife. I remember him also saying that she was his best friend and partner in crime, whatever he meant by that."

Oom Piet smiled. "Well the best to both of them," he said as he raised his glass, "they deserve their happiness."

"Did you know them?" the young man asked.

"Yes," Oom Piet said. "I knew them both very well, but that was a long time ago, long before you came to Brakenstroom."

The young man looked at Oom Piet, who was looking into his wine glass and chuckling softly.

"Oom Piet," he said, "when you get that look, I know you have a story to tell."

"Well . . . yes," Oom Piet replied, "one day perhaps, but not today."

"Ach no, man, you must tell us," the young man demanded as everyone in the bar gathered around Oom Piet to hear one of his famous stories.

"No, not today," Oom Piet said thoughtfully. "I must say though," he continued, "that life is amazing and full of surprises, " and he shook his head, then looked at his eager audience. "But I will tell you one thing. You know that diamond bracelet that Hettie Henning wears?" They all nodded. "Well Hettie found it inside her husband's safe after he died. He must have bought the bracelet for his first wife, but I never ever saw her wear it. Her name was Christa. I wonder whether he ever gave it to her." He rubbed his chin with his hand. "Well, at least he left Hettie with something. Pieter was at one time a very rich man, but he pissed most of it away on booze and gambling, and when he died, he left Hettie with very little, poor thing." He picked up a glass, rinsed it, and started polishing it.

Then he mused, "I suppose the bracelet is Hettie's now. Truly, she needs it; you know the old saying, Finders, Keepers."

A Child's Prayer

My Mother told me
Dear God,
That I have an Angel,
Dear God.
Where is my Angel?
Dear God
I need my Angel.

My father warned me
Dear God
That there is a devil,
Dear God.
Please keep it from me
Dear God.
Will you protect me?

My teachers taught me
Dear God,
That there is a heaven
Dear God.
Where is this Heaven?
Dear God
Is home my Heaven?

If I have an Angel
and You have the Devil
and home is my heaven,
Then why
Dear God,
Is the Devil let lose
To wander at will
And murder and kill
And all in a name
Dear God,
Your Name?

And where is my Angel
If you have the Devil
and home's not my hell.
My Angel
Dear God,
That holds me so close
That warms and protects
And keeps me from harm.
And all in a name,
Dear God,
Your Name.

I don't understand
Dear God.
I am very confused,
Dear God.
Please, do explain,
Dear God.
Show me your plan.

And then, when I know
Dear God,
What You intend
Dear God.
Will hate then cease?
Please God
Let there be Peace.

Jacob Singer,
November 1998

About the Author

JACOB ASHER SINGER WAS BORN in 1935 in the small town of Potchefstroom, 72 miles west of Johannesburg, in South Africa. After attending school at the Potchefstroom High School for Boys, he studied Pharmacy at the Chelsea Polytechnic in London, England, qualifying in 1958 and returned to South Africa.

In 1960, he married Evelyn Jackson, and practiced successfully as a pharmacist for the next twenty-five years, retiring in 1985 and emigrating to Canada in 1992.

Brakenstroom is his first book of short stories, but he says, not his last. His ambition is to retire for the second time to a quiet spot on the BC coast, and write. "There are so many beautiful stories still to tell, about South Africa, that are not political." he says. "South Africa is a beautiful country, with a fascinating although controversial history, and if it can remain Western, and not fall into the 'Africa trap,' it will soon become the tourist Mecca of the world."

Although never politically active, Jacob personally met and knew many of the active players on both sides of the political fence. When threatened by the Security police for not giving them certain confidential information, he decided it was time to join his children in Canada.

After a lifetime of living in a country torn apart by politics and intrigue, he admits that he does find Canada rather boring.